Your Dinner's Poured Out!

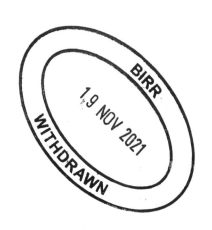

Paddy Crosbie on his last day at school, 22 December 1978

PADDY CROSBIE was born in Dublin in 1913, educated at St Paul's CBS, St Patrick's Training College, Drumcondra and University College, Dublin. He was the creator of radio and television programmes, including *The School Around the Corner, Back to School, Tug O'Words* and *Paddy's Playground*, and made frequent appearances on *The Late Late Show*. In 1979 Paddy Crosbie was honoured by Pope John Paul II with the Papal decoration Benemerenti. He died in 1982.

Your Dinner's Poured Out!

Memoirs of a Dublin that has disappeared

Paddy Crosbie

Introduction by
James Plunkett

THE O'BRIEN PRESS
DUBLIN

This edition first published 2012 by
The O'Brien Press Ltd,
12 Terenure Road East, Rathgar,
Dublin 6, Ireland.
First published 1981 by The O'Brien Press Ltd.
Reprinted 1982.
First paperback edition 1982.
Reprinted 1984 (twice), 1985.

Tel: +353 1 4923333; Fax: +353 1 4922777
E-mail: books@obrien.ie.
Website: www.obrien.ie

ISBN: 978-1-84717-304-1

British Library Cataloguing-in-Publication Data
A catalogue record for this title is available from the British Library

7 8 9 10 11 12 13
12 13 14 15 16

Printed and bound by CPI Group (UK) Ltd, Croydon, CR0 4YY
The paper used in this book is produced using pulp from managed forests

To My Wife, Peg

If you fulfil your longing
to return to your boyhood town,
you may find it isn't the town you are longing for;
it is your boyhood.   *Mark Twain*

CONTENTS

Introduction

The first School Around the Corner programme came on the
air in Radio Eireann in 1954 and it was shortly after that,
as Assistant Head of Drama and Variety, that I met its
schoolteacher creator, Paddy Crosbie. Six years later we were
working closely together on it to create its visual format for
Telefis Eireann. It was to become the first show of all to be
pre-recorded for the new television service, (Paddy arrived, I
remember, with a new blazer and the letters S.A.C.
embroidered prominently on its breast pocket) and it was
still top of the TAMS when it was discontinued over five
years later.

In the meanwhile, through several journeys around the
counties of Ireland and hundreds of recordings in towns large
and small, I grew to understand the qualities and individuality
of the show's originator. Paddy Crosbie had a rare gift for
presenting with precision and clarity the world of childhood
and children: their sense of fun; their varied and often highly
impressive talents; their ultimate and moving innocence.

To do so required in Paddy himself not only a depth of
sympathy and understanding but a precise and clearsighted
power of recall in the matter of his own childhood and
schooldays. This, of course, is a quality he has in abundance and this precisely is the quality he has brought to the
present book. To it he has added the fruits of his lifelong
study of his native city, so that he has been able to recreate
with accuracy and insight the gait of going of Dublin in
the 1920s.

And what a gait of going it is. Here is a world of lamp--
lighters, bootmakers' shops, Guinness barges with funnels
which collapse to allow them to get under the bridges; street
rhymes, rag-and-bone men, shunting trains and runaway
horses. Here was a city where the crowded streets were still

8

very near to the country – as near, at times – as the pigs and the hens in granny's backyard: 'Our entire district had a strong agricultural air about it during my boyhood. Unlike boys from the other parts of Dublin, we were in daily touch with the people from the farms of Meath, Kildare and Co. Dublin. The Haymarket was held twice weekly and farmers with hay loads as high as fifteen feet were arriving in Smith-field and Haymarket itself from early morning . . . Queues of haycarts formed at the six weigh-houses and Tony, Kevin and myself loved to wander up and down through these long corridors of yellow hay. Horses and farmers were very patient and the selling of the crop was done at a leisurely pace. Later in the day, when all of the hay had disappeared, some of the empty carts were left at the sides of both streets . . . With the farmers out of sight we children took over the empty carts.'

Another vivid picture brings us to Bow Street: 'There is one particular side-show of the Jameson distillery which has disappeared: I refer to the queueing of horses and carts at the entrance to Duck Lane for the left-over wash. This had an unmistakeably unpleasant, sour smell. Men came from far and near to collect grain and wash, both of which were given to pigs and horses . . . The grain was warm to the touch and on cold mornings the steam rose up from the many buckets of wash . . .'

In fact the predominance of horse traffic was very much a feature of that lost world: 'There were many different types of horse-drawn vehicles: drays, lorries, traps, hackney or side cars, long cars, cabs, brakes and floats. When the Lucan Dairy milk cars arrived on the scene they were compared with the ancient chariot. The rear was open and the driver just jumped on the back. The popular dray was a two-wheeled affair with a trapdoor in the centre. The driver was able to sit with his feet down on the axle underneath. Most drivers wrapped sacks around their lower quarters. The cabbies always did this.'

The other feature of Dublin transport was, of course, the electric trams; from four wheeled ones to the Dalkey and Howth lines which were eight wheelers; from the unassuming open top to the covered top with balcony ends, to the completely covered saloons and then to the glory of the

9

luxury tram which was the special pride of the Dalkey line.

YOUR DINNER'S POURED OUT brought that whole era back with all its teeming variety: the street characters, the slang and the sayings of those times; the bellows reddening the coals in the blacksmith's fire, the farriers, the coach builders, the aytin' houses, Phoenix Park and Knockmaroon, Christmas pantomime and the voice of the coalblock man and the bell on his cart sounding out in the dark stillness of a winter's night.

No better company in which to contemplate that world than that of Paddy Crosbie. And to wonder afterwards how it could have slipped away so utterly and so entirely, yet so quietly that it had gone before we noticed. Gone physically, that is. The ghosts are innumerable.

James Plunkett

THEATRE ROYAL

STAGE:

PADDY CROSBIE

IN

THE SCHOOLS AROUND

WITH

MAUREEN POTTER

WILL CARR AND PARTNER

ALICE DALGARNO AND BABS DE MONTE

THE ROYALETTES

JIMMY CAMPBELL and the THEATRE ROYAL ORCHESTRA

TOMMY DANDO

SCREEN:

JAMES DARREN and LAURIE CARROLL

IN

RUMBLE ON THE DOCKS

THE WATERFRONT GIVES ANOTHER GREAT
STORY TO THE SCREEN

A Walk Around
the Markets Area

*Oxmantown Green and the Green of St. Mary's Abbey —
The River Bradóge — Stoneybatter — Arbour Hill —
Smithfield — St. Anne's Well — Church Street — Newgate
Prison — St. Michan's Park — The Blue Coat School — St.
Mary's Abbey — Little John — The Four Courts — Sackville
Street.*

OXMANTOWN GREEN lay to the west of the Green of St.
Mary's Abbey, the two Greens combined stretching from
Capel Street to Stoneybatter. This was the Markets area of
my young days. The only part of the old Oxmantown Green
still remaining is the large playing-pitch behind the old
building, which is still known as the Blue Coat School. This
is now the headquarters of The Incorporated Law Society.
The building dates back to the days of Charles II of England.

In 1192 the district of Oxmantown was referred to as
Houstmaneby. It was a Danish settlement, the Danes having
moved over to the north bank of the Liffey, after the
Norman invasion. After Clontarf, they appear to have been
left undisturbed in their town of Dubh-linn at Christ Church.
The church of St. Michan was built in 1095, and it is generally
accepted that St. Michan was a Dane. The word Tolka is
also Danish.

Today the two Greens of Oxmantown and St. Mary's
Abbey embrace the Haymarket, Smithfield, the old Cattle
Market, the Fruit and Vegetable Market in Mary's Lane, the
Fish Market of St. Michan Street and the old Daisy Market.
Before stone and concrete appeared, a small river, named the
Bradóge, which means little salmon, meandered down from
Cabra across the Green and into the Liffey. Today, after
rising in Cabra, it reaches the top of Grangegorman, flows
down to, and under, St. Brendan's Hospital, turns eastwards

to the Broadstone, down the middle of Henrietta Street, turns slightly west down Bolton Street, under St. Michan's Park and Halston Street across Mary's Lane, down by East Arran Street, past Ormond Square and into the Liffey near the Four Courts. The earlier name for Arran Street was Boot Lane.

North Brunswick Street was formerly Channel Row, a name which is still retained in the Irish version, Rae na Canálach. The channel is said to be a tributary of the Bradóge. There is a large pool or pond underground, in the vicinity of Bow Street's north end. This may have a connection with the stream from Brunswick Street. The name of the pool was Loughbuoy or Loch Bwee, which means Yellow Pool. The word Buí or Bwee may have changed to Bow.

Broadstone is said to have derived from a huge stone which divided the flow of the Bradóge into two channels.

Stoneybatter (or Stoney-boher) meaning Stoney Road is a well-known part of Dublin. The name is a mongrel one, the original, purer title being An Bóthar Clochach (Boher Clockuk). Stoneybatter is 1700 years old and no street in Ireland can surpass that. It was the last place in the city where Irish was spoken. This was two hundred years ago, when the traders and shopkeepers had to use Irish to cater for the farmers and their families from the Meath Gaeltacht. The agricultural aroma of this part of Oxmantown Green made its presence felt in the entire district.

Aughrim Street used to be part of Blackhorse Lane, while Prussia Street was called Cabra Lane. The building of the North Circular Road in 1768 resulted in the formation of Aughrim and Prussia Streets. Stoneybatter itself was a one-sided street facing west originally. There was a large village green here, where a maypole dance was held every May. There was a riot on the village green in 1773, when soldiers tried to pull down the maypole.

Up to 1845, the only streets running west from Stoneybatter were Arbour Hill and Chicken Lane. Manor Street was part of Stoneybatter before this. On Arbour Hill there was a popular hostelry, which was famous all over the city for a drink called 'Apple D'Or'. This was during the eighteenth century.

There were stories (and are still) about subterranean

Thundercut Alley.

passages leading from Arbour Hill to Smithfield, and these were said to have been used by a famous thief, Scaldbrother. The name Scaldbrother was Danish, as was Fairbrother. Arbour Hill was Billy in the Bowl's territory, well-known in song and story. Constitution Hill was the site of a village long ago. The name was Glasmenoge.

Smithfield was and is a very wide thoroughfare, and as well known as Stoneybatter. All the lanes leading from Smithfield had names with farmyard undertones, all dating from the time when the Dublin Cattle Market was held there. There was Stable Lane, Duck Lane, Carters' Lane, Red Cow Lane etc. Between Duck Lane (now closed) and Carters' Lane (now Friary Avenue) there is still a well, situated behind the red-bricked houses on the east side, on Jameson property. The water in the well has a saline taste, and is thought to have some connection with the Liffey, which is about one hundred and fifty yards away.

On the west side of Smithfield there is a passageway, which bears the mystifying name of Thundercut Alley. This derives from a brewery — Thunder's — which was situated in the present New Church Street in the 1600s and early eighteenth century. Workers in the brewery, from the Stoneybatter area, used take a short cut to Smithfield; the short cut came to be known as Thunder Cut. When houses were built the right-of-way remained to become an alley-way.

Red Cow Lane got its name from a tavern situated in the lane at an earlier date. At the south end of Smithfield lay West Arran Street. This led from the quays to Haymarket. Today, it is a much shorter street. Also at the south end of Smithfield and facing into New Church Street near Thunder's Brewery was the town house of the infamous Lord Leitrim. This building was used in later years as a girls' school.

Moving east from Smithfield we come to Anne Street. Joe Brady of the Invincibles, was born in Number 22 here and attended St. Michan's Boys' School. I have been shown a deep well on Jameson property on the west side of Anne Street. This may well be St. Anne's Well, from which the street got its name.

St. Michan Street was called Fisher's Lane originally; this was where the fish market was born. On the south bank of

Smithfield and Markets Area of 50 years ago.

16

17

the Liffey facing this market was (and is) Fishamble Street, which also had a fish market. The now well-known Chancery Street was Pill Lane. Pill may mean poll (a hole) or pool, from the Bradóge, possibly.

St. Michan's Church is the oldest and best known church on the north city side. Besides the famous vaults there is a grave outside, supposedly that of Robert Emmet. The Church is one of the first places to which tourists are brought. The organ on which Handel is said to have played is a great attraction of course.

Church Street, originally Oxmantown Street, was the main thoroughfare on the north bank up to the end of the 16th century. It had attáined this position in a natural way, as it was the first street encountered after crossing Whitworth Bridge from the south side. This bridge was the connecting link, across the Liffey, with the walled town of Dublin.

A long lane grew from the Bradóge to Stoneybatter; this was called King's Lane. Today it is known as North King Street. There were two Poor Clare Convents in or near this street at one time, one of them near Red Cow Lane. There was also a medical school here on the sites of St. Patrick's National School and the Christian Brothers' School of Channel Row. It was in this medical school that Lady Tyrconnell died in 1730.

One cannot but notice the over-use of the term 'lane'. Many of the present-day streets of Dublin were dubbed lanes up to the Twenties. There are very few lanes nowadays. The lane in which I lived, changed from Bridewell Lane to St. Thomas Terrace; at the present time it enjoys the title of Arran Quay Terrace.

Near North King Street there is a cluster of streets, the names of which — Lurgan, Lisburn and Coleraine — recall the building of the Linenhall structure in 1726 and its strong ties with the Ulster industry. The 'new' Newgate Prison close by was built in 1774, beside Green Street Courthouse. It was built to replace the 'old' Newgate Prison at Cornmarket. The prison lasted until 1893, and from its ashes rose the present St. Michan's Park, which was opened by Michael Davitt.

There were underground passages leading from the prison into the courthouse. One side of the courthouse looks out on Halston Street, which was originally called Bradóge Lane. Beresford Street — or to give it its local pronunciation, Barefoot Street — commenced its life as Frapper Lane. Nearby Stirrup Lane did not derive from the harness piece, but from the name of a family.

Retracing our steps and crossing Smithfield, where Michael Moran or Zozimus, the famous blind ballad singer, lived for a time, we reach Queen Street. This street is named after Queen Elizabeth I of England, after whose death in 1603 an order was made 'that part of Oxmantown Green be taken and set in lots for farms, reserving a highway (Queen Street) and a large market place (Smithfield)'. Two hundred years ago Queen Street must have been a beautiful place with its tall Georgian buildings, but surpassed of course, by the wide Blackhall Street, which played the role of a very wide avenue leading to that splendid piece of architecture, The Blue Coat School. And why shouldn't this area feel important? Wasn't the Irish Parliament (?) held here in 1729, when the building of Parliament House in College Green commenced? Benburb Street, close by, was named Barrack Street at first; the eastern half of it was called Tighe Street.

Down on the quays was Queen's Bridge, also called Bridewell Bridge. The bridge at Winetavern Street was named Richmond Bridge. Francis Higgins, the sham squire, notorious informer, lived at 20 Usher's Quay, facing St. Paul's Church (1785). This part of the Liffey is said to be the exact site of the Ford of Hurdles from which the old Gaelic name of Dublin derives. Edmund Burke, the famous orator, was born near St. Paul's on Arran Quay, at Number 12. The family moved to Ormond Quay at a later date.

Over on the near south side were Dirty Lane, Dunghill Lane, Mullinahack, Hell, Murdering Lane and Cut-throat Lane. Dirty Lane was that part of Bridgefoot Street nearest to Thomas Street, while Dunghill Lane was one of the alleys running west from it. Mullinahack, originally an Irish name, Muileann a' Chaca, was the name of a mill — the dirty mill — and was sited a short distance south from the Brazen Head Inn. Hell was to be found at the north-west corner of Christ Church. Murdering Lane was the old name for Cromwell's quarters and Cut-throat Lane was nearby. Pigtown was to be found off Basin Lane.

Let us return to the north bank again. We can walk along Pudding Lane to Hangman Lane (Hammond) and on to Petticoat Lane, off Mary's Lane. Here we are reminded of St. Mary's Abbey founded by the Cistercians, the only part of which still standing, is the Chapter House, where Silken Thomas threw down his sword in 1534 in his first gesture of rebellion.

The Cistercians laboured in the Abbey for five hundred years, until dispossessed at the time of Henry VIII, although they held on for some time. The old Abbey is still remembered in the names of the surrounding streets — Mary Street, Abbey Street, May Lane, Little Mary Street and Mary's Abbey Street. Very few Dubliners know the exact site of the Chapter House. It now lies seven feet below street level. The green of the ancient monastery is recalled in the names Green Street and Little Green Street.

Oxmantown Green and Arbour Hill had a link with Robin Hood and his gang of thieves. When the 'merrie men' were scattered from Sherwood Forest, Robin's right-hand man, Little John, came across to Ireland. It is said that he demonstrated his power with the bow and arrow by sending a single arrow from Whitworth Bridge to Arbour Hill. However, Arbour Hill was to see the end of him, because, at a later date he was hanged there for sheep-stealing. He was able to cod the Sheriff of Nottingham, but the Dubs of Stoneybatter were not impressed.

The earliest settlements on or near Oxmantown Green by the Danes were those of Glasmenoge, Grangegorman and Oxmantown itself. Glasmenoge was situated in the Broadstone-Constitution Hill area. The name Grangegorman derived from Gormo, King of Denmark (died 930 A.D.). Stoneybatter, although older than Dublin itself, remained a streeted village for centuries. There were no large edifices on the north bank of the Liffey until the Royal Barracks (now Collins' Barracks) were built in 1701.

The Four Courts were completed in 1796 on the site of the former Dominican Priory. Then came a spate of buildings — Gandon's King's Inns, the Broadstone, the G.P.O., Jervis Street Hospital and Rutland Square (now Parnell Square). Drogheda Street, which had been a long narrow lane, and which came to a full stop at the Liffey, was re-designed by

Luke Gardiner. This new street — Sackville Street — became the show-piece of the capital. As O'Connell Street at the present day, it can hardly be called a show-piece. My parents always referred to it as Sackville Street.

At the turn of this century Dublin was still a rather small city. It was encircled by two very long roads, the North Circular Road on the north side and the South Circular Road on the south. Beyond these two semi-circles lay that vague place called the country. We, as children, called all those, who lived in, or came from, the country areas by the single word 'bogmen'. On the north-side, Cabra was deemed part of the country, as was Finglas, Santry, Ashtown etc. There was nothing to be seen but fields of grass everywhere.

Paddy Crosbie, Christmas 1913.

1 Roots

*Our street — My parents — 'Your dinner's poured out' —
O'Donovan Rossa and Kevin Barry — The family — Rents —
Bare feet — First playmates — 'My' Dublin.*

I WAS BORN in a jail. Well, actually, that is not true; what is true is that the walls of the building, where I made my first personal appearance, had been the walls of the old Smithfield Bridewell. The address was 12A Bridewell Lane and the lane ran from Smithfield to Queen Street and led on westward to Benburb Street. The house was exactly one hundred and eight boy's steps from the River Liffey itself.

Our home was the old 'two up, two down'. The stairs faced the front door, which opened on to Burgess Lane, which in turn led to the Haymarket. Two of our windows looked out on one lane, while the remaining two faced on another. All of which means that the house was a corner house. Nothing extraordinary in that, of course, but it was common local knowledge that Edward VII, on one of his many visits to Dublin, as Prince of Wales, was found 'maggoty mouldy' drunk in O'Connell Street by an innocent policeman, and was arrested and lodged for the night in my Bridewell home.

Local tradition had it also, that our house was situated at the rear of No. 4 Haymarket, one of Robert Emmet's depots on the North City side in 1803. The Bridewell itself had been built in 1756 and was used for about a century and a half. The building was demolished in 1979.

My mother and father came from Wexford town. My father, Martin Crosbie, was a foreman-fitter and turner on the Permanent Way, that is the tracks section, of the old Dublin United Tramways. Before coming to Dublin, he had earned quite a reputation in his native town, both as a singer and comedian. He won the Wexford Feis gold medal in 1904 in the tenor competition.

My mother's father was a printer named John Corcoran who, before leaving Wexford, and in partnership with his brother Willie, founded the once well-known Wexford newspaper, *The Free Press*. My mother's mother, a farmer's daughter, was a Stafford from Rathaspick and my father's mother was a Bolger. She was reputed to have had a three-octave voice, and used sing in Bride Street Church in Wexford.

My birth coincided with the start of the big 1913 Strike and, of course, the First World War was just around the corner. My memory of the big strike is practically nil except what I picked up from my mother, when she spoke of those hard times. This was really a time of great poverty, a poverty which lasted right through the '14-'18 War. Bread and tea was the menu for *all* meals. 'Johnny, come in here this minit; your dinner's poured out'.

I would say that eighty per-cent of the people of Dublin of that time were poor, very poor. All the well-paid jobs were held by Protestants. And most of the big businesses were owned and run by them.

'How is your mother, Tommy?'

'She's fine, Mrs. C.'

'And did your father get a job yet?'

'Sorta, Mrs. C! He's sellin' furniture.'

'Oh, that's great! And is he doing well?'

'Oh, very well, we've only the bed left now!'

Besides giving us a short-lived taste of poverty, those early years also gave us a taste of life in Ireland under British rule and my own resentful feelings on this subject have never left me. My mother built up these feelings also by what she said and did. When I was two, she carried me to Glasnevin to be present at the funeral of O'Donovan Rossa. And when Kevin Barry was hanged in Mountjoy Jail in 1920, she brought my brother and myself to join the great Rosary-chanting crowd outside.

The eldest in our family was my brother, John Martin, who was called John in school, Mossy both at home and on the street, and later Martin, when he was making a big name for himself as a singer. My only sister was named Margaret;

however, she was always called Mona. My younger brother Gabriel Peter, did not arrive on the scene until 1922. He was called Gerry by everybody. I, myself, was christened Patrick Harold, and so I was called Harry for a time. I opted for Paddy as early and as quickly as possible. At home, they called me Harold, a name I have always hated. My mother's name was Elizabeth, but she was always called Lily. Name-changing seems to have been the fashion in our family.

I can remember an incident that happened when I was two. My father had forgotten to put the little barrier gate at our front-door. This had been made specifically to keep me in. Anyway, I toddled out, turned the corner of Bridewell Lane and made my way to the end of the path at the corner of Smithfield. Standing and looking across what seemed a huge expanse of roadway, I saw horses standing outside a place near the entrance to Stable Lane. I made my way across the wide roadway and stopped near the horses. The place itself was a forge, and I can remember the sparks flying. Just as I was moving closer to get a better view, I was whipped up by my mother, who bore me home, as if I had been away for weeks.

I mention this because it is my first and earliest memory. The memories that follow closely on this incident are confused and hazy and are composed of running people, games, soldiers, gunfire, lorries, policemen, shouts of 'Shut that window!' and a man crying like a child.

As I mentioned before, everybody seemed to be poor; our parents were all working-class. Our family was lucky to be living in a rented house on our own. The rent was five shillings during the War and was raised to eight shillings afterwards. The rent for two rooms in one of the Queen Street tenements ranged from two shillings to four. Although some of the rooms had an air of poverty, many people managed to keep their homes beautiful. However, in the poorer ones, one heard what was to become a music-hall joke: 'Now, Tommy, don't spill anythin' on the table-cloth, your father hasn't read it yet.'

Many of the boys and girls were barefooted. In the summertime we all went barefoot by choice; it gave a sense of freedom and seemed to add to our speed in running. However, when the colder weather arrived, we were glad to get

Paddy's mother Elizabeth (Lily) Crosbie.

back to boots. Boots were more popular than shoes; why, I don't know. Black runner shoes made of rubber were popular also; they always exuded a clean smell of tar, and a boy could run very fast while wearing them.

The first boy I ever played with was Kevin Costelloe. He was a small, fair, curly-headed boy, who was slightly younger than myself. I remember that he wore a bib, a garment commonly worn by small boys in those days. He lived on the first floor, over the Sweeneys, in Number 9 Haymarket. On that first day, we played with a large cardboard box owned by Kevin. I pulled him down along the path to St. John's public house at the corner of Queen Street and he pulled me back to the corner of Burgess Lane. On returning home at mid-day, I gave a breathlessly detailed account of all that had happened. The world seemed a rosy place indeed. I was three at this time and the Rebellion was over.

My second playmate was a boy of about the same age. He was Tony Mangan, who was fair-haired also, and always wore a gansey. His father was the local barber, and had his shop at the corner of Bridewell Lane and Queen Street. Tony was adventurous and full of life, and we became great friends. His father's shop was always crowded and a story went the rounds about a little dog that came each day and sat watching one of the assistants at work with the scissors. It seems that one day the dog had got a piece of ear.

Late playmate arrivals were brothers, Paddy and Hobby Stynes, who resided over the Cork Dairy in Queen Street. Paddy was the elder, fair-complexioned and good-looking. As brothers, they spent a lot of time quarrelling with each other. One day they were fighting in Burgess Lane. My mother opened our door and called out, 'Stop your fighting, Paddy Stynes. If you don't, I shall tell your mother. Who started it?'

Paddy (pointing to Hobby): 'He started it when he hit me back.'

The size of that first small gang began to swell. A younger boy joined the ranks not long afterwards, a small tubby fellow by the name of Philip Fitzsimons, whose father was a postman. Then came Michael Lyons from No. 12 on the north side of the Haymarket. His father had a hackney jaunting car. My brother, Mossy teamed up with George Kane from No. 8, who was of the same age. There were others of their age group, of course, all big boys, but the only time we joined forces was when we were playing street games. Other pals of Mossy were Archie Corr, Jamesy Devine and Ritchie Fogarty.

As I said before, the lane where I was born and the streets in which I played were all situated on Oxmantown Green. The major streets of my Dublin in the Twenties were Stoney-batter, Smithfield, Church Street, Capel Street and the North Quays. I include also streets of the South side, lying near the Liffey, such as Thomas Street, High Street and Bridgefoot Street.

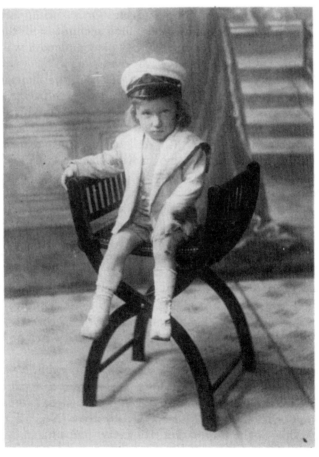

Mossy in 1913.

2 Early Days

Stealing hay — Horses and horse-troughs — The mystery parcel — Street-shouts — The watering car — First day at school — Going home — Proddy Woddies — Hymns.

BEFORE I WENT to school, I remember being intrigued with the actions of a group of boys who used go 'on the jare' every Tuesday and Friday, the two haymarket days. As laden haycarts passed along Bridewell Lane, on their way to Smithfield, some of the group ran out and pulled an armful of hay each. All of this hay was piled near the corner of Burgess Lane. I learned afterwards that they sold this hay to some of the back-lane 'farms' that abounded in the district. Sometimes, of course, their hay-pulling was noticed and an angry farmer waving a stick shouted 'If I lave my hands on you, I'll cut the arse off you'.

As small children we played some simple pranks and games. We loved to play at the horse-troughs, particularly the one in Haymarket. There were two others in Smithfield. Splashing the water at each other was our idea of fun, but of course this always angered the drivers of the many horses that came to quench their thirst. It was wrong, of course, but on hot summer days, it was lovely to sit on the edge of the iron trough and splash water with the feet. A very angry driver would shout: 'If yez don't get away from that water I'll take your sacred life.'

The whole world was full of horses then. Delivery cars, milk-cars, lorries — they were all horse-drawn. On Tuesdays and Fridays, when the farmers arrived with their hay-loads, Smithfield and Haymarket reeked of horses. The smell of fresh horse-dung and horse-piss filled the air, and nowadays, whenever one of these odours strikes my nostrils, my mind flashes back to the horse-packed, hay-packed, farmer-packed scenes of Smithfield long ago.

One of our favourite pranks was to make a neat parcel with paper and twine of some horse-dung. Leaving it on the path we hid behind a corner and we hugged ourselves with delight, when anyone picked up the parcel and opened it. Most of the victims laughed, when they heard us laugh, but there was one big man once who chased Tony Mangan and myself as far as the Phoenix Park, he was so mad.

Other early childhood pranks included shouting advice at certain grown-ups. To a man on a high bicycle we shouted, 'Hey, mister, get down off that wall! Here's the gardener!' Or to anyone on any kind of bicycle we sang, 'Hey, mister, your wheel's goin' round', or 'Your back wheel is follyin' your front.' And of course we sang the inevitable, 'What do you feed your mother on?' after the bell-man, and hugged ourselves with sheer delight when he answered, 'Coal Blocks! Coal Blocks!'

Hot dry summers brought the Corporation horse-drawn watering cars out on the streets to keep down the dust. We young children, in our bare feet, followed the spraying rear of the cart. Now and again, the driver pulled down the lever full tilt and an umbrella of water enveloped everyone. Even the driver himself seemed to enjoy the shouts and screams of the children. It was a happy time. 'Hey, mister, do it again! Aw, go on, *please*!'

At the age of four I went reluctantly to school in Stanhope Street Convent. My mother came with me the first day, but I looked after myself after that. Sister Lawrence was the Mother Superior, and the lay teachers were Miss McDonald, Miss Doherty and big Miss Dunn. There was also Sister Lioba, who prepared me for my First Confession and First Communion. I liked school after the first day and I can remember that the little red-haired girl who sat beside me on my very first day was Mary McHenry. Before that first day, I had been very much afraid, but it turned out to be a nice place.

Going to and coming from Stanhope Street Convent was always an adventure, particularly on Cattle Market day, which fell on Thursday. This was the day when large herds of cattle and flocks of sheep padded their way down Stoney-batter. Most parents came with their children on that day.

The children were terrified when a bullock broke loose. The 'cow-up' call of the stick-armed drovers plus the barking of the sheep-dogs and the lowing, bellowing and baa-baaing of the animals made an exciting scene.

One day a big bullock got wedged in the door of Connell's pub and a carpenter had to be brought to cut through part of the upright. I loved the cleverness of the sheep-dogs, as, with tongues hanging out, they padded from right to left behind their drover-owners, waiting for a whistled or shouted order, to tear away to the front or side of the trotting flock. How I longed for a sheep-dog of my own. 'Hey, mister, give us that oul' bowler.'

Coming home from school we stopped to look into Laheen's shop, to see boots being made or repaired. The barber's shop also had a fascination for us, so we used push open the door of Kearns Hairdressing and watch, in wonder, as the man with the razor quickly made the face of the man in the chair come into view. Then, as Mr. Kearns made a run at us, we hurried on to stop and gaze at the comics and pictures in the window of Cahill's, the newsagent, near King Street corner.

I came home, always, by the Protestant School in Blackhall Parade. These pupils were let free about half an hour after the closing of our school. As I came by I often heard them singing British songs,

'Pack up your troubles in your old kit bag
And smile, smile, smile.'

And of course I heard them singing,

'It's a long way to Tipperary
It's a long way to go.'

And because I knew the air I recognised, 'God Save Our Glorious King'.

We never learned songs like these in the Convent School. We were taught plenty of hymns e.g. 'I'll sing a hymn to Mary', the Lourdes Hymn and a hymn which we all thought was 'Oh Mother I could sweep the earth', but which in reality was 'Oh, Mother I could weep for mirth'. We learned also 'Sweet Heart of Jesus', 'To Jesus' Heart All Burning', 'Hail Glorious, Saint Patrick' and so on. We knew all of these songs and sang them lustily on the many occasions offered, particularly at the May Processions.

After school our childhood games and pastimes around 1918 and 1919 were occasionally interrupted by the sights and sounds, and even smells, of the everyday life of the small world of north-west Dublin. Quite often the sounds of a fight caused boys to pause and listen: 'Go on now, me brave fella, I där yeh. Hit me now with the child in me arms'. This would have been a row between husband and wife.

There were times when we paid scant attention to the shouts and screams, and although they did not hinder our simple games, the phrases and accents constantly assailed our ears, reaching and touching us lightly yet not affecting us unduly. The only time we left everything and ran was when the cry went up: 'Rucky up! Rucky up! Rucky up in Hentown!' This always meant a fight between two men, and that was always worth watching. A drunken man would peel off both coat and shirt, throw them on the ground, pull up imaginary sleeves on his bare arms, and standing out in trousers only, invite another to fight him. 'Come on now, yeh hoor's get! Come on now and I'll bate the shite outa yeh.' There was more sparring done than actual fighting and much of the time was spent by friends holding back the belligerent one. 'Let me at him! I'll massacree him!'

Fights between women with shawls always took place in the middle of the roadway. The preliminaries consisted of a good deal of hand-slapping and repetitive name-calling, culminating in a question like 'Who was it had a military weddin'?' This was the signal for real action. Suddenly shawls were thrown aside and the two went for each other's hair, screaming and cursing at their most feminine pitch.

All this, and more, formed the ingredients that went to make the rich, fruity cake of our early years.

3 Family, Friends and Neighbours

*Our house — Earthenware jars — Neighbours — Mr. Dooley —
Grannie Corcoran in Phibsboro — Joe Nolan's phonograph —
Aunt Katie of Cork Street.*

NONE OF THE HOUSES in the district had electricity. My
mother had a gas-stove for cooking; she also used the range.
The light was the old gas-mantle type, but we used oil lamps
too. Candles were used also; the large ones cost one penny
and there were ha'penny ones as well. I loved the candle;
by staring at the flame one could see pictures. About 1924
my father arrived home with a new kind of light, called the
Coleman Quicklite. It worked like a Primus Stove, that is, it
had to be pumped. There were two mantles on it and a
reflector, all of which gave a very bright light. There was one
snag — it roared just like a Primus.

My mother kept our house shining clean. The range
gleamed, particularly at night in the gas light. There was a
long sofa under the kitchen window and the table stood in
the centre. By the side of the stairs was our cabinet, which
was painted mahogany. The sink with one cold tap was in the
corner farthest from the front door. In the other corner was
the door to the backyard and toilet. My father roofed half of
the yard and this was used as a pantry. One bedroom was
over the kitchen; the other was over the parlour.

In the winter, we had no such luxuries as electric blankets
and rubber hot water bottles had not made their appearance
yet. Earthenware jars were used and because they could
become very hot indeed, a large stocking or woollen cloth
was wrapped around them. 'Ma, this jar is leakin'.'

There was no such thing as carpet on the floor. We had
linoleum on all of our floors, even on the stairs. There was a
cheap type of lino available but some people were able to

Grandparents John and Elizabeth Corcoran, about 1910.

boast about their inlaid lino, which, of course, was dear. In our house we had unusual looking mats. They were made of a rope fibre, and were very strong and long-lasting. My father got them from Wexford, where they were made by the lighthouse men on Tuskar. 'Wipe your feet; I'm only after polishing the floor.'

The lino in our parlour was bought at the door from an Indian by my mother. I think she paid one pound for it. Indian pedlars were very common in Dublin and were to be seen carrying rolls of lino from door to door. We often wondered how they made a living. They never minded us children shouting after them 'Hey! Sore Head'.

The parlour was our best room. It lay to the right as one came in the front door. We had a large hanging clock there that was made in Massachusetts, and it chimed every quarter hour. Facing the window there was a piano — a Crane and Crane — which my father often played. He couldn't read music and always played by ear, but he did enjoy playing and singing. There was always singing around the house; Martin was always singing and I did my share of it. My mother had a good voice, but never sang on her own; her forte was harmony. She could harmonise naturally with any singer.

The parlour was our special room for visitors, but it was used also by ourselves at Christmas time and on special occasions. As I mentioned before, the parlour window looked out on Bridewell Lane and for as long as I can remember, there had been an aspidistra in the window. I believe my mother got it from her own mother. Every other house had an aspidistra; it was the custom.

Next door to us lived the Woods family, and next to them were the Wests, the only Protestant family in the street. Our three houses together formed what had been the Bridewell Station. The police barracks itself had been in Phoenix Street, the back entrance to which opened on to Stable Lane. As boys we heard the big house in Phoenix Street referred to as the Barracks, but we never knew why.

As very young children we often stood outside a particular house in Bridewell Lane and sang:

'Mr. Dooley,
Done his pooley,

Up against his sister's garden wall;
His sister caught him,
And smacked his bottom,
And poor ol' Mr. Dooley done it all.'

The chase by the man concerned was the exciting bit; but one day a bucket of water stopped us for quite a while.

The Smithfield Motor Company was really situated in Smithfield then, near Stable Lane. There was a Ford car in the showroom window. It was shiny and new and the price tag on the windscreen was in large figures, which I remember clearly: £105.

Every Sunday when the weather was fine my mother brought us either for a walk to the Phoenix Park to hear the band in the Hollow, or to our grandmother's house in Phibsboro'. On our way to Grannie Corcoran's we walked along the bank of the Royal Canal from the Broadstone, after crossing the Viaduct, of course. This was a great treat as there were ducks in the canal here. I can still hear my sister chant an old rhyme.

'Grandmother, grandmother Gray
May I go out to play,
I won't go near the water
To hunt the ducks away.'

There was a footbridge across the canal half-way between Broadstone and Blacquire Bridge. Blacquire Bridge was a hump-backed one and going over it in a tram was quite a thrill, as the rear of the tram used swing upwards when crossing the apex, and throw everyone forward. 'All hands on deck, we're goin' up a hill.'

I loved the visits to my grandmother's; her house faced the old Bohemian Cinema. She had a garden and kept hens, and it was my delight at this stage to collect the eggs. My grandfather smoked clay pipes and used put the old used ones in the gutter of an old coal-shed in the garden. I gathered these unknown to the others and used them for blowing bubbles. Somehow I liked the stale tobacco smell from them. And besides, I was able to swop them for marbles on Mondays.

My grandfather became white-haired as he was growing old, but my grandmother kept her dark hair until she died. She had a very gruff manner, but was very kind and gentle

Aunt Katie and Uncle John (Murray) of Cork Street on a Sunday jaunt.
Also Grandmother Corcoran, Mossy and Aunts Nellie and Annie.

Paddy's father, Martin Crosbie.

behind the rough front. My mother's sisters' names were Minnie, Annie, Cissie, Katie, and Nellie. Her two brothers' names were John and Pat.

Aunt Minnie lived in Fairview and was married to Joe Nolan, who had a good position in the fish firm of Hanlon's of St. Michan Street. To reach Aunt Minnie's house we took the No. 23 tram along the quays. This turned at Capel Street Bridge, turning again into Parnell Street. The terminus was at Ballybough Bridge, whence we walked through a passage-way with upright anti-traffic barriers, on to Cadogan Road where the Nolans lived.

Uncle Joe had a huge collection of stuffed birds in glass cases, some of which were very large. There were falcons, eagles, owls and small birds like linnets, finches and robins. I never troubled to find out why or where he got them. However, what did interest all of us, and my father in particular, was the phonograph in the parlour. This was the fore-runner of the gramophone. Instead of discs or records, there were cylinders. My father was enchanted with the machine, and listened with delight to singers like John McCormack, Ernest Pike, J. C. Doyle and Walter McNally. Those were the four names that I heard mentioned as my father and Joe Nolan talked and argued. Popular songs were 'The Moon Hath Raised', 'Come into the Garden, Maud' and 'There is a Flower that Bloometh'. Another seven or eight years were to pass before my parents bought our first gramophone in Kearney's of Capel Street, a H.M.V. cabinet model.

My mother's sister, Aunt Katie, lived in Cork Street at No. 130. Her husband's name was John Murray; he had a chandler's shop. On visits there, I was often shown the tenement house opposite, where Joe McGrath of the Irish Sweeps had lived. The rear garden of Murrays was very large and in it there was a huge dilapidated shed. As children, Mossy, Mona and I loved to go exploring and as there were so many nooks and crannies, it was ideal for playing Hide and Seek. Murray's house itself was a very old one, a late Georgian type. The rooms were very large and there was a hall entrance apart from the shop. Addie was the eldest son, and the next to him in a family of six was May. Addie did most of the serving in the shop and I often envied him as he sold candles over the counter or measured out a quart of paraffin oil. He was still attending school, of course.

The walk from our house to Murray's, which, of course was in the Liberties, was full of interest. Crossing the bridge from Queen Street we started up the hill of Bridgefoot Street. At the bottom of the hill, there were always huge horses with fine manes and hair-spatted hoofs. These were used to help other horses of the firm bringing some of the Guinness barrels up the steep hill. My father jokingly told me on the first occasion that these gigantic animals were Shetland Ponies and I was nearing twenty years before I discovered the truth. They were Clydesdales and were beautiful animals to behold.

On the right-hand side of Bridgefoot Street were tenement houses and yards. I distinctly remember a name, 'Freely and Son, established 1710', over one entrance to a timber yard on the right-hand side going up the hill. The street was much narrower at this time.

Reaching Pimlico, we never walked around the well-known semi-circle path, where there seemed to have been an eternal toss-school, and where once there had been a drinking fountain by the wall. Instead, my father led us to a short-cut, by going a little way up South Earl Street to an alleyway between tenement houses. The next item of interest was the Pimlico playground here, which had swings and slides and many other amusements. I wished we had had one in our own district.

John Murray was terribly keen on cycle-racing and attended all the sports meetings, no matter where they were held. Two of the big names in Uncle John's estimation were Bertie Donnelly and Herbie Breadon. Everybody went to the Tramway Sports in Jones's Road, now Croke Park. There was a cycle track around the edge of the pitch, and it was always very exciting as the last lap approached. The races were mostly handicap. One runner we all admired was a man named J. J. Ryan from Tipperary, who never seemed to lose. In handicap races, it was thrilling to see the way he overtook his rivals in the Four Miles. I remember reading an article by J. J. in *Our Boys* in which he gave some unusual advice regarding health. 'Drink water', he said, 'as much and as often as you can.'

4 Agricultural Dublin and its Side-Shows

The Haymarket — Aytin' houses — See-saw — Saddlers and Farriers — Pigs and hens — The long cars — Queen Street tenements — Piersse's School — The hot wall — Grain and mash — The mail-car — The fire-brigade.

OUR ENTIRE DISTRICT had a strong agricultural air about it during my boyhood. Unlike boys from the other parts of Dublin, we were in daily touch with the people from the farms of Meath, Kildare and County Dublin. The Haymarket was held twice weekly and farmers with hay loads as high as fifteen feet were arriving in Smithfield and Haymarket Street itself from early morning.

The men from the hay factors were always 'on the stones', that is, out on the roadway, to meet them. The men I remember were Jim and Matty McAuley from 7 Haymarket, Mr. Keane of Dodds, Larry O'Neill and Larry Cuffe from Smithfield, men from Wilkinsons and Cartons, plus one or other of the principals of McKeown and McKeogh. Larry O'Neill was Lord Mayor of Dublin at this period.

Queues of haycarts formed at the six weigh-houses and Tony, Kevin and myself loved to wander up and down through these long corridors of yellow hay. Horses and farmers were very patient and the selling of the crop was done at a leisurely pace. Later in the day, when all of the hay had disappeared, some of the empty carts were left at the sides of both streets. The horses from these carts were being fed in different yards around the place. The owners made their way to one of the many aytin' houses for a meal. Church Street and Benburb Street had an abundance of these aytin' houses. The most popular one was that of Conroy's in Benburb Street. The smell of rashers and eggs from this place would make you hungry, even if you were just after a good

No. 7 Haymarket, The McAuleys (1916).

Dodd's of Smithfield.

meal. This was after the war of course, from 1919 on. There was another well-known aytin' house at the north end of Smithfield named Doggets.

With the farmers out of sight we children took over the empty carts. They made ideal see-saws, as the protruding prongs at the rear were about half the length of the shafts. Tony, Kevin, Philip and myself, perched at the four corners of one cart, see-sawed the happy hours away until the return of the owners. Sometimes the farmers returned, not from a meal, but from one of the pubs, St. John's, Minogues or Keogh's. 'Look out! Here's the man!'

To cater for the farmers and their horses there were forges, coach-builders, saddlers, wheelwrights, seed shops, butchers, poultry shops and shops with farming implements. Scanlan's, the saddler in Haymarket was a very popular place and we loved to look in and watch Mr. Scanlan working on a harness. The smell of leather always attracted us; it was such a clean smell.

The forges fascinated us. The two Byrne brothers had their forge over by Stable Lane. I thought then that the blacksmith was the greatest man on earth. Only a great man could take up the hind-leg of a young horse and slice and rub and prepare the hoof for the coming shoe. Tom Byrne often allowed us into the forge and on one occasion he let me pump the bellows. I have never forgotten that.

Tom Byrne picked a long strip of iron, put the end of it into the furnace, then broke off the required amount for a shoe. Next with a tongs he put the cut piece into the furnace again, and then he and his brother shaped out the shoe on the anvil with the hammer. The smell of burning hoof made me cough, and I always looked at the horse to see if he felt the hot steel.

The flying sparks as the hammer struck the red-hot metal turned the forge into a fairy-land. Then when the shoe was finished, it was shoved into a huge tub of water, making a sizzling sound, of which I was reminded, when I heard the hiss of a snake for the first time. The forge in the Haymarket was owned by Bill Walsh; afterwards a Tom O'Loughlin took over.

Church Street, King Street, Stoneybatter and Arbour Hill and many other streets had back-yard farms. Pigs were reared and fattened in all of these places. Float cars were a common sight in the streets as boys or young men went from house to house looking for slop for the pigs. 'Slop! Any slop! Slop!'

Mr. McAuley of the haymarket, the hay factor, also kept pigs in a yard in our lane. These were tended by a young man named Matty Brazil, a fresh-faced, good-humoured, young man, who always whistled at his work. The other boys, Tony, Kevin, Philip and I often watched him cleaning out the byres; they were always spotless, and particularly so after Matty had given the walls a coat of white-wash, which was often.

There was a coach builder at the corner of Haymarket, the north-west corner. The name over the gates was James Doyle & Son, Coach Factory. The building stretched half way up the Haymarket and all kinds of horse-drawn coaches were made there. The Doyles and Bourkes supplied the 'Long Cars' for the many outings of the Queen Street community. These took place on Sundays or Bank Holidays and all the adults seemed to go on the trips. Another well-known coach builder was Moore of Brunswick Street.

The outings were to the Strawberry Beds usually, and on one occasion to the Scalp, near Enniskerry. The day (we heard afterwards) was spent drinking and singing and dancing. The excitement and bustle in Queen Street on the morning before departure was infectious. Now and then, a giddy horse caused a commotion with a sudden move forward. The few not travelling, stood at the hall-doors, or arm-folded themselves at the windows: 'Mind yourselves now! Don't do what Francy did! Watch that Jemser coming home. Keep him up straight or he'll spill some'. Poverty was forgotten. Sure wasn't 'Uncle' there with the three brass balls? What about the Trouble? What Trouble? Haven't we troubles of our own? No matter how late they returned some insisted on dancing on the street. Up the Rebels!!

In all of the Dublin parishes in the Twenties a house to house collection was made by special collectors. The collector for Arran Quay was an ex-altar-boy named John Hanway. John was a tall, fresh-complexioned fair-haired boy from Stoneybatter. His area was Queen Street and on many occasions I went with him to help. A rap at each door brought one of the occupants of the room quickly enough to

Strawberry Hall Pub in the Strawberry Beds.

find out who was there. Over the shoulder was shouted
'It's the Arran Quay man.' 'There's a penny on the cabinet
under the tumbler. Give it to him.' The frying-pan was heard
from some rooms, while the smell of pig's head and cabbage
came from others. The former were the late risers, the
latter the early ones. The collection was made about 10.30
a.m. or 11 o'clock. I helped on those occasions, when I
wasn't scheduled to serve Masses.

The shouts and noises of the tenements were very O'Casey-
like in one way, but I never once heard the people of Queen
Street use the flowery poetic language used in *Juno* or *The
Shadow.*

The doors of most tenement houses were left open all
night. The stairs were areas of pitch darkness. In many of the
King Street and Queen Street houses there was only one flush
toilet for the entire house and this was sited in the yard. The
houses were Georgian-style with basements. In Blackhall
Street the houses were four-storeyed over basement.

There was no talk during my boyhood days of the now
famous saintly Dom Marmion, who was born in Queen
Street. The name of Cooper, however, was known all over the
city to those interested in horses. Bourkes, the undertakers,
was always a big name in the district. Almost facing Blackhall
Street was Dicky Piersse's school. The official name of this
school was St. Paul's Free School. This name is still on the
walls that remain today. Catherine McAuley, the foundress
of the Sisters of Mercy, lived for a time at No. 52. The 1916
martyr James Connolly also resided in Queen Street in the
early days of this century. The boys who attended the Free
School sang a song:
> 'Dicky Piersse is a very good man,
> He goes to Mass on Sunday,
> He prays to God to give him the grace
> To bate the kids on Monday.'

The school was made up of two tenement houses merged
into one. Mr. Coyne and Mr. Crean were teachers in the
school during this period.

The washing of doorsteps and window-sills was a great
old Dublin custom. This was always done on Saturdays, in
preparation for the Sunday. The work was done, of course,
down on the knees with hard brush and soap and the custom

46

Bourke's the Undertakers of Queen Street.

still prevails in some areas like May Lane and Beresford Street. However, as many steps and sills are now painted or coloured, the work is not as laborious. The scrubbing of window-sills was done in the Twenties even in the tenements, and of course the sills had to be very clean, what with the washing flapping around on the triangular line, which was a feature of all tenement windows.

One very noticeable characteristic of most of the tenement rooms was the large amount of furniture. There was always a huge sideboard, cluttered with all kinds of ornaments and statues. Each statue had a protective glass covering. A statue or picture of the Sacred Heart was to be found in every room.

'And how would you recognise Our Lord if he was walkin' down Queen Street?'

'That's easy — He always wears his heart outside of his shirt.'

The stone setts or cobblestones were on all the roads in the city. We used to call the stones durlogues and of course, the traffic was very noisy, what with iron-rims on all wheels. However, outside of hospitals, one found wooden setts, which were put there to deaden the sound of passing traffic. These wooden setts were to be seen outside the Richmond Hospital and the Mater until the Fifties.

There are very few cobblestones to be seen in the city nowadays; the modern roads are much more even and easier to clean. The stone setts persist however in areas like Smithfield and the Haymarket. In fact, I remember one single stone, which had tar on it in the early Twenties. Recently, while walking through Smithfield I saw the same stone in the same spot with the same blob of tar on it. It hadn't changed in fifty years.

There are other things and places in the Markets area, which have changed very little during that period; I refer to firms and buildings. Just as the firm of Arthur Guinness and Son dominated, and still does, the south-west side of the Liffey, so too did the well-known firm of distillers, John Jameson and Son, dominate the north side in the Markets area. The distillery covered a huge acreage and played a big part in my early life. We played football and handball in Bow Street and there we heard about the famous Hot Wall. This was part of the distillery wall facing May Lane. The heat attracted many 'down-and-outs' of an earlier time during the winter months. The wall became heated from the furnace inside.

Originally called the Bow Street Distillery, it was working as a distillery in 1780, and the Jameson family acquired an interest in it towards the end of the century. By the year 1810, it had passed into sole possession of John Jameson, from whom the firm got the world famous name. The Jameson wall in Smithfield was one of the many I climbed and ran along with companions, who were just as daring and foolhardy as myself. 'If yeh don't come down owa that, I'll break your arse with trips.'

There is one particular side-show of the Jameson distillery which has disappeared. I refer to the queueing of horses and carts at the entrance to Duck Lane for the left-over wash. This had an unmistakeably unpleasant sour smell. Men came from far and near to collect grain and wash, both of which were given to pigs and horses. I do not know when this activity stopped, but as far as I can remember, it always took place on Thursdays. The grain was warm to the touch and on cold mornings the steam rose up from the many buckets of wash. Some men used to fill a barrel with the wash; these barrels seemed to be part of the carts and had taps on them. The grain was distributed with the shovel by a Mr. O'Connor.

The mail-car was another feature of our neighbourhood. After leaving the G.P.O. it careered up Henry Street and Mary Street, clattered its way through the narrowness of Mary's Lane, turned into Bow Street, then New Church Street, and it was at this point it came into view. It was a two-horsed lorry with caged sides, inside of which stood one man surrounded by mail-bags. The two horses galloped madly, while the driver stood up and used his whip. It was in every way like a speeding chariot, except for the four wheels. Tearing across the waste ground of Smithfield, it rattled its noisy way through Bridewell Lane, then on to Benburb Street, on its way to the then Kingsbridge Station. I often saw the speeding horses foaming at the mouth and judging from the speed of the mail-car, it must have been racing against the clock every time. Anyway we all wondered why it travelled so fast; there were no pursuers. On its way back, the horses came at a gentle trot and presented a complete change from the outward journey. However, the greatest thrill of all for small boys was the horse-drawn fire-engine. The sight of those galloping horses plus the clanging of the bell as the helmetted driver steered his way through Smithfield to a fire in North King Street is something I shall never forget. In the darkness sparks were flying as the iron wheel-rims met the cobblestones.

Bow Street Distillery, Dublin.

5   Rhymes and Chants of the Twenties

'Brokenhearted, Brokenhearted' — *'Feck, damn, blazes'* —
'Specky Four-eyes' — *'Dicky, Dicky Dout'* — *'Holy Moses'*
— *'Billy the Barber'* — *'Icky Ocky'* — *'Old Mrs. Bellybum'*
— *'Will I tell you a story?'* — *Once on a time'*.

AT SIX YEARS I was growing up and I knew it. Just like all
the other boys who played on the streets and around the
tenements I learnt and chanted rhymes and sayings, some of
which were not nice, to say the least. We also told funny
stories to each other over and over again. Like the one
about the Scotsman, who was found dead in the lavatory in
O'Connell Street, with a suicide note:
>'Brokenhearted, Brokenhearted,
>Paid a penny and only farted.'

That really made us laugh. Then there was the old parody on
'The Old Apple Tree', which we sang loudly for everyone to
hear — except our parents.
>'In the shade of the old apple tree,
>Poor Mary got stung by a bee;
>She was milking the cow,
>But she didn't know how,
>So she started by tickling its knee.
>The cow took its foot from the grass,
>And gave Mary a kick in the arse;
>Poor Mary fell,
>And the cow ran like hell,
>In the shade of the old apple tree.'

And there was the old puzzle: 'Riddle me riddle me this; how
is it a hen can't piss.' Another chant of ours as youngsters
was a list of so-called curse-words. This was chanted to an
air similar to that of the Rakes of Mallow. It was a single line
and was repeated over and over.

'Feck, damn, blazes, cocky, piss and snots,
Feck, damn, blazes, cocky, piss and snots' and so on.
We did this to shock the grown-ups and indeed Mrs. Cullen told the story to my mother and I paid the penalty. The custom was kept on, of course, and for all I know the present day boys may be chanting it.

One song we all knew was 'Down by the River Sawya'. Our pronuncuation of the last word was most unlike that of present day singers. Our version, I would say, was the correct one. Also, in one of the verses of the present day there comes the line 'Two poleese an a 'tective man' — The original version was 'Two poleese and a pólis-man'. And of course, there was the Limerick, unrepeatable, which commenced, 'There was an old woman, God bless her' . . . .

The boys always kept together and never mixed with the girls, except when the barrel-organ man came around. We all danced to the music then. Sometimes when the girls were skipping with a large rope, we used to run in and skip, but this always ended with some mother coming out and ordering us away. I remember the girls chanting:
'Paddy on the railway
Picking up stones,
Up came the engine
And broke his bones;
"Ah" says Paddy
"That's not fair"
"Ah", says the engine
"I don't care." '
When we saw a boy coming out with sugar on a slice of bread we said:
'Sugar Babby, Sugar Babby
One, two, three.'
To a boy with spectacles we shouted, 'Specky Four-eyes!' To a boy with long hair the phrase was 'Hey, Starve the barber!' To a man with a beard 'Hey, Beaver!'

The girls always played Beds outside Mrs. Cullen's shop, because they felt they were safe from the boys there.

When we saw any boy, big or small, with torn trousers we chanted after him:
'Dicky, Dicky Dout,
With his shirt sticking out,

Four yards in,
And five yards out.'
The girls also shouted this after any boy, when they were
wanting to be chased.
   Other rhymes were:
     'Kennedy's bread would kill a fella dead,
     Especially a fella with a baldy head.'

     'No more English, no more French,
     No more sittin' on the cold hard bench,
     Bang the table and knock the chairs,
     And throw the Master down the stairs.'
The above was chanted on the day we broke up for holidays.
Another one went like this:
     'I've got the toothache,
     A gumboil, the belly-ache,
     A pain in my left side
     And a pimple on me bum.'
One of the nicer ones was also chanted:
     'One, two, three, four, five, six, seven,
     All good children go to Heaven,
     When they die their sins are forgiven
     One, two, three, four, five, six, seven.'
I cannot remember why we sang this one:
     'Tramp, tramp, tramp, the boys are marching,
     Cheer up, the Bobby's at the door,
     If you do not let him in,
     He will break the door in,
     And you'll never see your Mammy any more.'
We often heard the girls at their games chanting:
     'Charlie Charlie, Chuck, chuck, chuck,
     Went to bed with two oul' ducks,
     One duck cried, the other died,
     Charlie, Charlie, Chuck, chuck, chuck.'
It never made sense to the boys and it is still a mystery to
me. Although there were no Jews in our neighbourhood we
sang:
     'Holy Moses, King of the Jews,
     Bought his mother a pair of shoes;
     When the shoes began to wear,
     Holy Moses began to swear;

When the shoes were all wore out,
Holy Moses began to shout.'
Another chant which my mother did not approve of was:
'I think, I think, I smell a stink,
I think, I think, I do,
I think, I think, I smell a stink,
And I think it's off of *you*'
This one used to vex Tony Mangan, because his father was a
barber:
'Hurrah for Billy the barber,
He went and shaved his father;
The razor slipped,
And cut his lip,
Hurrah for Billy the barber.'
Another rhyme which comes back to me was:
'The boy stood on the burning deck,
His feet were full of blisters,
His father was in the public-house
And the beer ran down his whiskers.'
Everything seemed to have a rhyme:
'Ice cream a penny a lump
The more you eat the more you jump.'
I remember also:
'I've a pain in me belly
Said Doctor Kelly
Rub it with oil
Said Doctor Doyle,
A very good cure,
Said Doctor Moore.'
There was one short question and answer rhyme, which went
like a Gregorian chant:
'How is your oul' wan? Game ball!
Out in the backyard, playin' ball.'
When we wished for rain, we chanted together:
'Rain rain come down,
And I'll give you half a crown.'
In wet weather we changed it slightly:
'Rain rain go up,
And I'll give you half a cup.'
Whenever we wished to find out who was to be 'on it' in any
game, we stood around in a circle and one boy pointed at

54

each of the others one by one as he chanted:

'Icky Ocky,
Horse's Gocky,
Icky Ocky
Out!'

Whoever was pointed at on the word 'out' was 'on it'. We also used the rhyme 'I think, I think I smell a stink' for this purpose. On other occasions we used the old reliable: 'Eeny Meeny Miny Mo etc.' There were other rhymes besides those for starting games. There was:

'Train, train number nine,
Run along a crooked line,
If the train goes off the track,
Do you want your money back?'

The boy at whom the finger was pointed answered: 'Yes, fourpence'. The 'finger' boy then counted one, two, three, four. The boy at 'four' was 'on it'.

There is only one other of these rhymes that I can bring to mind:

'Old Missus Bellybum,
Fell down the telyfum
How many miles did she fall?'

The answer, e.g. five, six, or seven, helped the final picking of who was to be 'on it'.

Yarns about Paddy the Irishman we just loved. Paddy was driving his ass and cart along with vegetables and met a woman. 'Do you want any carrots or peas?' said Paddy. 'Oh' said the woman 'I haven't had a pea for forty years'. And said Paddy 'Gee-up, Neddy, there's goin' to be a flood'. Every time we told that story we laughed.

Whenever we saw the sign 'Post no Bills' we automatically set up the chant:

'Post no bills, play no ball,
Kiss no girls behind this wall.'

Meeting a rival gang, members of each warned the other with H.O.H.A. which meant 'hit one, hit all'. It always helped to settle the situation. However, if a fight commenced, fists only were used. It was quite unthinkable to kick anyone, and if a boy fell to the ground his opponent waited for him to rise. It was an unwritten law. If a boy was reluctant to 'stand out', that is to fight, the watchers always shouted to the

Smithfield (waste ground) from Haymarket.

opponent: 'Go on, give him the coward's blow'. In the case of a boy refusing all invitations to fight, the onlookers chanted 'Cowardy Cowardy Custard'.

Bigger boys used say to the smaller fry:

'Will I tell you a story?
About Johnnie Magory?
Will I begin it?
That's all that's in it.'

or 'Shut your eyes and open your mouth, and see what God'll send you'. Sometimes a dead fly or maggot was put on the tongue. And there was of course that ominous rhyme which when invoked usually had the desired effect:

'Give a thing and take it back
God will lash you down below.'

The smaller children had a rhyme of their own:

'There was a little man,
And he had a little gun,
And off to Candy's he did run;
With his belly full of fat,
And a big tall hat,
And pancakes hangin' from his bum, bum, bum.'

The sight of a TO LET sign always tempted us to fill the gap to produce the full word TOILET.

Although my memory is running short of these rhymes of the street, phrases linger on like 'goin' for the milk in the oil-can' or 'Green, White and Yella, You're a lovely fella.' Then we also heard about 'the back o' the pipes, where the spiders walk on crutches.' This was near Dolphin's Barn.

The lowest name one could be called in my young days was 'a corner-boy'. The real corner-boy hung around corners, but grown-ups applied the term to all youngsters who formed into groups or gangs and shouted insults and rhymes after their elders.

'What's your name?' (Grown-up's question)
'Butter and Crame, (Cheeky answer)
All the way
From Dirty Lane.'

Towards the end of the war, in 1918, we were singing songs that came over from the trenches:

'Mademoiselle from Armentieres, Parley Voo,
Mademoiselle from Armentieres, Parley Voo,

Mademoiselle from Armentieres,
Hasn't been kissed for forty years,
Inky Pinky Parley Voo.

The Prince o' Wales is gone to jail, Parley Voo,
The Prince o' Wales is gone to jail, Parley Voo,
The Prince o' Wales is gone to jail,
For ridin' an ass without a tail,
Inky Pinky Parley Voo.

Up the stairs and into bed, Parley Voo,
Up the stairs and into bed, Parley Voo,
Up the stairs and into bed,
Throw your oul' wan over your head,
Inky Pinky Parley Voo.'

There was another song which came back from the Front, but which is best left out. It certainly could not be mingled with children's rhymes.

There is one particular rhyme which keeps coming back to me and although it is a coarse one, I think I should set it down lest it be forgotten:

'Once on a time, and a very good time,
And a very good time it was,
When dogs shit lime and very good lime,
Yes, very good lime it was;
And the houses were all thatched with pan-cakes,
And the streets paved with tu'penny loaves,
And little pigs ran round in the streets,
With knives and forks stuck in their arse,
Cryin' out: "Who'll ate me?" '

The last few lines do not rhyme, but that is the way I remember it.

We had a recognised shout for gathering the gang. First out on the street let out a continuous sing-song shout of:

'Oo-ah, Oo-ah,
All the gang
Oo-ah, Oo-ah,
All the gang.'

And of course to finish off a game the cry was 'All in, all in, the game is broke up'.

6 Religion in Boyhood

*First Communion — The priest in Dublin life — May and
October Devotions — Scuttin' the trams — May procession
— Sunday morning — Fr. Aloysius and Confession —
Confirmation — The Catechism.*

I MADE MY First Communion at the age of six years in
Aughrim Street Church. My First Confession was a night-
mare, which remained for me a long time. The Confessions were being heard in the red-bricked Convent chapel
attached to Stanhope Street, and we were brought there by
Miss Doherty, Miss McDonald and Sister Lioba. 'And don't
forget to say your Penance'.

I wished to tell the priest that I had cursed a number of
times, but I felt that the word 'curse' was itself a curse and
that I couldn't possibly use it in the Confessional. The priest
was rather cross, and told me to leave the box and return,
when I was ready to tell my sins. I didn't go back to him
and spent a most unhappy day in the playground later.

First Communion was different. It was a most happy day.
After the ceremony, we were given tea and biscuits in the
convent by the nuns. That day my mother took me and the
rest of the family to my grandmother's in Phibsboro'. Aunt
Annie brought us to the Blacquire Cinema, the 'Fizzer',
and we were treated to Vimto and ice-cream. My grandfather gave me a whole half-crown for myself. Every single
person seemed to be my friend on that First Communion
Day.

We were taught in the convent school, and later in the
C.B.S., to respect the priest. When meeting a priest on the
street our usual salutation was:

   'God bless you, Father'
   'God bless you, my child.' (his answer)

Older boys with caps raised the peak, just a fraction, as a sign of respect. Boys with no caps raised fringe or forelock, while little girls actually genuflected while addressing the priest.

Confession was a weekly Saturday afternoon affair and the most popular priest in the whole district was the famous Father Aloysius in Church Street. His 'box' was the first on the left near the altar-rails. We went to him because he was so very quick. It was said that at times a boy was seen to come out of each of the two sides at the same time. The big disadvantage was the long queue.

'Bless me, Father, for I have sinned.

It's a week since my last Confession and I said me Penance. I disobeyed me mother twice, I cursed ten times, I called old Mr. Murphy names and I stuck to last week's school money an' told the Brother I forgot it.'

'For your Penance say one Our Father and ten Hail Marys. Now say a good Act of Contrition: Absolvo te etc.'

Coming out of the Confessional Box I made my way, like everyone else, up to the altar-rails to say my Penance.

'What did he give yeh?'

'One Our Father and ten Hail Marys'

'Janey, he gev me the very same.'

One day about fifty boys were waiting for Confession in Church Street. There were about six full rows of us, all waiting for Father Aloysius. When Confessions commenced the boys were going in and out of both sides as if there was no priest in the Confessional. Then there was a hold-up due to Hobby Dunn. Those of us near the box could hear the two voices.

'Father, I fecked apples.'

'You what?'

'I fecked apples.'

'What do you mean — you fecked apples?'

'I - I - I fecked apples.'

'I don't understand you.'

At this point Hobby opened the door of the Confessional Box and asked us: 'Give us another word for feck'. We shouted together 'RAWB' (rob). Hobby closed the door and finished his Confession. Fr. Aloysius, Fr. Dominic and Fr. Albert were the three priests who attended to the 1916

Leaders in Kilmainham Jail. The late evening Confessions were reserved for adults.

Mother: You won't be heard at night.

Small boy: Sure I can shout.

Our mothers sent us to the May and October devotions, which consisted of Rosary and Benediction. I was brought to the October Devotions in Church Street in a group led by Nellie Costelloe, who was much older. At the bottom of Carter's Lane (Friary Ave.), we used look in at a huge furnace in Jameson's. It was the last grilled window on the right and the blazing furnace was so bright and strong that someone said that it was Hell. And we believed it.

At six and seven years I was going to the October Devotions in Arran Quay without a chaperon. Our group went early and we spent the extra time scutting on the trams. The trams going towards the Phoenix Park were our choice because between Church Street Bridge and Queen Street Bridge the conductor was upstairs collecting fares. So we hopped onto the platform and enjoyed a jaunt up to Queen Street. 'If I catch one of yous, I'll redden your arse.'

We played games around the pillars that stand outside St. Paul's Church. On the stroke of eight, we scrambled our way upstairs to the gallery, where we knelt or sat the time away. I didn't realise that very soon I was to leave all this and take my place down on the altar itself. At this time my thoughts on Benediction were a little off-beat. My definition of the Monstrance was 'It's the thing the priest lifts up and peeps through at all the people'. The bright lights inside of the church were in strong contrast to the gaslight and candles at home.

The May Procession was a very strong Dublin custom. Stanhope Street Convent claims to have inaugurated it in Ireland. Anyway, it spread through the country and the regular hymn was the Lourdes hymn. Many people were weak in the verses, but everybody came in strongly on the Ave.

Ave, Ave, Ave, Maria
Ave, Ave, Ave, Maria

In St. Paul's Church all children taking part assembled in and around the Baptistry. The Confraternity men, led by Danny Maher, policed the whole proceedings. Adoring parents waited in the church seats for the appearance of their children, and I actually saw mothers cry as we passed by. The route was a longish one to us, down one side aisle and up the other, finishing up on the altar. 'Gawney, will you look at them; aren't they lovely?'

In other parishes, the procession was an outdoor one, depending on the weather. In our parish there was no place near the church for such a ceremony. The talkies, radio, television, singing pubs and football matches on Sunday all combined to give this lovely custom a deadly blow.

Saturday night was bath night, or wash night, in every house. Heads were scrubbed, ears were washed and those going to Communion fasted from midnight. Boots were polished — in our house this was done by my mother. Shirts were laid out ready for the morning. I can remember waking on Sunday morning to the joy-bell peals of bells from John's Lane. The gay sound of these bells came across the Liffey to us on the north side and gave Sunday morning an extra-special something.

The sound of something frying on the pan belonged to Sunday also. After the war years and the Treaty when life was beginning to be a little rosier, a rasher and sausage was a great treat. On Sundays, my father seemed to wear a dark brown suit always. The most popular colour was navy blue. These could be bought for £2; a flannel trousers cost five shillings, and an extra good one seven and six. 'Look at him, all dressed up like a dog's dinner.'

The next important step on the road to Heaven was Confirmation. Mossy received Confirmation in the year 1921 and I 'made' mine in 1924. There was an unwritten rule that a boy or girl had to be ten years to be considered by the examining priest. My mother brought Mona and myself to Mossy's Confirmation in Arran Quay. The Church was packed with boys and girls from 'Brunner', St. Patrick's School in North King Street, Piersse's School in Queen Street and the Girls' School in West Liffey Street. 'All parents up on the gallery, please.'

In 1921 the National feeling was evident everywhere and fifty per cent of the boys wore kilts, while many girls wore Celtic type dresses. Mossy wore a kilt that day and I remember how well he did on our rounds afterwards to our

Mossy in Confirmation kilt (1921).

relations. My sister Mona was confirmed in St. Michan's Church in Anne Street, because in 1923 she was a pupil at the Presentation Convent, George's Hill. My turn came the following year and once more my mother headed for St. Paul's, Arran Quay with Mossy and Mona. We marched down from the school through Smithfield on a bright sunny day. Once again half of the boys wore kilts. I wore a suit made of dark blue material.

'I'll remember Confirmation Day
Until the day I die;
We made it on last Tuesday
An' the sun was in the sky.
The skeule was shut an' the day was free,
An' the roads were clean an' dry —
I'll remember Confirmation Day
Until the day I die.'

Missing the Catechism was the worry of every boy. There was the small Catechism or Penny Catechism and the Large Catechism, which cost three ha'pence. Pages of answers had to be memorised, and shortly before the big day the local examining priest came in to test everybody. Boys who were weak in Catechism were put back, and had to wait another two years. On account of this, some boys left school without receiving Confirmation. Whether the system was right or wrong I wouldn't like to say, but one thing is certain — we knew our Catechism. It was parrot-like yes, but even to this day, the answers from that old Catechism book come easily to my mind. Some of the funny answers remain in my mind also. 'Fifth: Thou shalt not kill. Sixth: Thou shalt not milk a donkey.'

7 The Daily Scene

'How are the tomatoes, Paddy?' — *Cadging apples* — *Grannie Fogarty's hens* — *Second-hand clothes* — *Pawn-brokers* — *Harry Lipman of George's Lane* — *Lar Whalen's crocks* — *Cowtown* — *Shoe-shine boys* — *Runaway horses* — *Horse-drawn vehicles* — *The funeral.*

THE FRUIT AND VEGETABLE Market in Mary's Lane was another place for exploration. Here again, we saw the farmers and growers bringing in their produce on horse-drawn carts. Like the hay-men, they came from Counties Dublin, Meath and Kildare. Horse-dung filled the roads outside and the passages inside the market. A Corporation man spent all the day cleaning up with shovel and brush. We loved the shouts, the noise and bustle and we often listened in on a bargaining session:

    'How are the tomatoes, Paddy?'

    'One and nine a chip, Maggie me Darlin' '

    'You have your glue; they're only one an' a tanner in Fletcher's.'

    'Look at them tomatoes, the best redskins you ever saw. You won't get those for one an' a tanner anywhere. But as it's yourself, Maggie, one and eightpence.'

    'Now don't hurt yourself. I wouldn't give more nor one and seven.'

    'Oh, alright, but it's losin' money I am with yous people.'

We always managed to get a few apples.

    'Hey, mister, gi's an apple.'

    'I'll give yez the toe of me boot.'

    'Aw, mister, that one there; it's goin' bad.'

Soon Tony, Kevin and I had a few apples each, and were on

our way home scutting behind a lorry. The lorry men were the best for giving scuts. They never seemed to mind up to a half a dozen boys on the back of the lorry. And it didn't seem to make any difference to the horse.

We found it hard to talk to each other when on a lorry. The wheels were iron-shod and as we rattled over the cobble-stones, every word had a shaking, quaking sound. Also the noise of the wheels made conversation impossible. However, we did not mind this; we covered a great deal of ground in those days on the backs of lorries.

I wish again to stress the 'farm' atmosphere of our whole district and one outstanding feature was the keeping of hens in every street. McKeowns kept hens, as did Grannie Fogarty in No. 9. I always made it my business to run up to Grannie Fogarty with a basin of left-overs for her hens. She never failed to give me a penny. Most of those who kept pigs also kept hens. There were many of such places around Arbour Hill, Stoneybatter, North Brunswick Street, Prussia Street, Oxmantown Lane, Church Street, etc.

All of which shows that this area of the city on the North side of the Liffey had a character of its own. It was the other side of the Dublin coin, because the people in the Markets area are as Dublin as those of the Liberties. For proof of this, consult the appendix on p. 218 giving sentences and phrases from my past and also providing a glossary of some Dublin slang terms.

The biggest market in the district was, of course, the Cattle Market. The area surrounding the Cattle Market was known locally as Cowtown. This name embraced Prussia Street, the North Circular Road, Manor Street, and Aughrim Street. The state of the streets and paths on market days is difficult to describe. It was impossible to pass through the area without getting one's boots coated with manure. Besides the cattle, drovers and sheep dogs, I was always intrigued by the many boot-polishers on the streets. These were boys and men who, armed with polish, brushes, cloths and foot-stools, took on the job of cleaning the well dirtied boots and leggings of the cattle buyers. Shoe-shine boys! 'The smell in that place would trip you up.'

These buyers were all alike. They wore wide-brimmed battered hats, two coats — the outside one being a rain-

N.C.R. bordering the Cattle Market.

The Dublin Cattle Market. (Large house on left is City Arms Hotel).

coat — brown boots and leggings. Every one of them carried a stick. Some cattle came to Dublin by train, but in the late Twenties the use of lorries became general. Some cattle and sheep arrived on Wednesday and were grazed overnight in fields along the Cabra Road. People nearby were always complaining about the bleating of the flocks of sheep all through Wednesday night. The pubs and boarding-houses never complained and the City Arms Hotel in Prussia Street and Hanlon's Pub saw the clinching of many a cattle deal. The City Arms was once the town-house of the Jameson family. The cattle market area at the rear had been their garden and orchard. The house is two hundred and fifty years old and is a typical Georgian mansion.

One outstanding feature of my Dublin of nearly sixty years ago was the large number of second-hand clothes shops near the Vegetable Market and Moore Street. There was a line of these shops in Mary's Lane, and Little Mary Street was just one mass of them. Nearby was the Daisy Market. Further down we had the second-hand clothes shops of Cole's Lane and Sampson's Court. Nearby were the Anglesey Market, Riddle's Row and the Rotunda Market. The presence of so many of these shops tended to emphasise the poverty of the period. Michael's Hill, just across the river, was another much frequented clothes market, and of course, there was always the Iveagh Market. 'The only thing that fat trollope can buy readymade is a handkerchief.'

Pawnbrokers were to be found in every district, recognizable by the three brass balls hanging outside their offices. There was a Mr. Hackett in Queen Street, who was succeeded later by Mr. Kearns. These shops were well-known; Gorman's, in Winetavern Street; Sohan's of Townsend Street, Andrew's of Capel Street and Fitzpatrick's of Ellis Quay. Monday was the busy day in the pawnship, when all kinds of articles from spoons to suits were pawned; they were redeemed usually on Friday or Saturday. There were other men, who carried on the business of buying and selling, but who were completely different from the pawnbroker.

Everybody knew of Johnny Fox in Bride Street, where one could get anything from a man-hole cover to a mongoose. On the north side in George's Lane, off Brunswick Street we had Harry Lipman, whose name for buying rags,

Sampson's Court 1922.

Old Anglesey Market near Moore Street (1918).

Rotunda Market — between Cole's Lane and Denmark Street.

bones, bottles and jam-jars was known far and wide. In the same business, but not as famous, was Danski, who had his pitch in North Brunswick Street itself, opposite Brunswick Villas. Both of these men built up a very lucrative business over the years, and their names were on everybody's lips. They bought other items besides the ones mentioned. I often saw the old-fashioned bedsteads outside of Harry's. 'Where did you get that — in Harry Lipman's?'

Another well-known name from North King Street was Lar Whalen. At Lar's one could hire a bicycle for a day for two shillings. They weren't very reliable models and so anyone seen riding around on a dilapidated bike was always asked 'Is that one of Lar Whalen's crocks'

Although the bicycle was coming into general use the horse was still king of the roads — the smell of horses was still strong up to the Thirties. With so many horses on the streets, runaways were to be expected. When the cry was raised 'Runaway horse! Runaway horse!' there was a scatter in all directions. Children were grabbed by parents and hustled into homes or shops or doorways. The sight of a runaway on a public street was frightening, to say the least. I remember one particular afternoon when I witnessed a brave act at close quarters. It was after school and I was standing at the corner of Red Cow Lane, before crossing over to Bergin's shop in Smithfield. A runaway horse, a young colt, came careering along King Street towards Smithfield. A D.M.P. man hearing the commotion took off his cape and running with the horse, he very expertly threw the cape over the animal's head. The horse stopped dead. The story was in the *Evening Mail* and *Irish Independent* the next day, and I was able to boast about witnessing the whole event.

Falling horses, particularly on frosty mornings, was another hazard. Everybody in those days seemed to have some knowledge of horses. As soon as a horse slipped or fell, a dozen or more helpers gathered around to prevent the beast from rising again, while under the shafts. Some held the horse's head flat, others loosened and opened the straps; then the shafts were pulled back leaving the frightened animal free to scramble to its feet. After this, the helpers melted away, each one about his own business.

Incidents such as these were very common and there

wasn't much excitement generated. Somehow or other, the horses belonging to the farmers, who came in with their hay on Tuesdays and Fridays, never seemed to be touched by these types of accidents. Their movements were always rather slow, and this may have kept them safe. In fact, it was common practice with many of the farmers to fall asleep in the cart, and rely on the horse to make his own way home. It would be foolhardy to do such a thing now.

It is easy to understand why many Dublin people of the present day find it hard to believe that there was such a Dublin forty, fifty or sixty years ago. I suppose life in the Markets area was comparable with life in a Provincial town. The horses and carts helped to create this atmosphere.

There were many different types of horse-drawn vehicles, drays, landaus, lorries, traps, hackney or side cars, long cars, cabs, brakes and floats. When the Lucan Dairy milk-cars arrived on the scene, they were compared with the ancient chariot. The rear was open and the driver just jumped on the back. The popular dray was a two-wheeled affair with a trap-door in the centre. The driver was able to sit with his feet down on the axle underneath. Most drivers wrapped sacks around their lower quarters. The cabbies always did this.

Mr. Sweeney, who lived in No. 9 Haymarket on the ground floor was the driver of a lorry and like Mr. Lyons, he often gave the children a jaunt around Haymarket. Oh, life was simple and good and so satisfying and we all loved horses. We loved them best of all when there was a funeral. Funerals were wonderful occasions for young boys and girls:

> 'Oul' Da Byrne is dead and is laid out at the top of
> Queeno. Are yez goin' up to see him?'
> 'When will the funeral be? Is he goin' to Glasnevin?'

Most funerals were delayed until Sunday, because the Brian Boru pub was a bona fide house, and could stay open until midnight on Sundays. We were never stopped at any of the wakes; children were always welcome. 'Go on in there now, son, and say three Hail Marys for his soul. And don't make any noise, sure yez won't.' Tony, Kevin and myself were always struck dumb at the sight of a corpse on a bed. The whispered conversation of the adults had a freezing effect on me, so after saying in a loud voice the phrase that covers everything – 'I'm sorry for your trouble' – I hurried home to find out if my mother was going to the funeral. She wasn't, but Mrs. Mangan was bringing Tony and would take me along. My mother didn't know the dead man. The funeral was horse-drawn, of course, and the horses looked grand with their black plumes. The plumes made them look taller, like circus ponies. 'Can we sit up with the driver? It's not goin' to rain. Can't we sit up with you, mister?' This was the part of the funeral we loved, the jaunt on the cab. Many of the cabs belonged to Bourkes, the Undertakers of Queen Street; the same cabs were used for weddings, for which occasions the plumes on the horses were white. Off we went from St. Paul's, Arran Quay, up through Smithfield, turning at North King Street and turning south again to pass the house of the dead man. Three times we went around the block, as was the Dublin custom. The blinds on all windows were drawn, and neighbours stood and talked and nodded on the footpaths.

'I wonder will he make the horse gallop?'

'Ask him, go on.'

'Mister, will you be galloping the horse soon?'

'He didn't hear you; ask him again.'

When we passed under the viaduct at the Broadstone, the horses began to trot. 'Go on, mister, race that one in front. His horse is an oul' nag.' At Doyle's Corner, there was another funeral coming up the North Circular Road. Our cab joined a big long line of cabs, that stretched from Doyle's Corner to the cemetery. The roadway here was a mass of steaming horse-dung. Tony told his mother that we'd wait with the cabby. 'Will it take long to bury him, mister?' . . . 'Can we hold the nose-bag to feed Charlie?' . . . 'Keep your head still, Charlie, or you'll get nuttin'.' After about an hour Mrs. Mangan and her friends came back. It took another half hour of shaking hands and talking before everybody sat in. 'Will you make him gallop now, mister?' Aw, go on, sure the funeral is over.' We didn't stop at the Brian Boru; we stopped at the Hut at Doyle's Corner. We promised the cabby to mind his horse and he went in with the rest. Mrs. Mangan came out with two bottles of Vimto. Yes, it was a great day.

I must have gone to a dozen funerals during the Twenties and not one of the deceased was a relation of our family. 'He got a good send-off anyway; I hope I get as good.'

One of Bourke's landaus at Punchestown (1917).

8 The Big Strike, Rising and Civil War

The Big Strike — The Citizen Army — The 1916 Rising in the Markets Area — 'Today is Ireland's Day' — Curfew — The Troubles — The Truce — The British Tommy leaves — The Irregulars in Smithfield — The fire in the Four Courts — End of the Civil War.

MY OWN EARLY boyhood and some major historical events range through the same years. By all accounts, the years between 1910 and 1920 were the years of the greatest poverty. Many married working men had less than one pound a week, and when the Big Strike started in 1913, it took great courage on the part of the poor working class to answer Jim Larkin's call. He had been born in Liverpool of an Irish mother. A very big man, I saw him at three meetings, when, without the aid of microphones he seemed to mesmerise the attentive crowd, with both voice and arms.

I have rather hazy memories of 1915 and 1916, but I do remember the venom of some men as they spat out the words of 'Scab' and 'Blackleg' for years after the strike itself. These names passed on later to sons and daughters.

The working man of 1913 was beaten in the end by the bosses, but when the pains and the pangs of the birth were over, the baby called Trade Unionism began to take its first unsteady steps. Today, it is a fully grown giant.

Before he went to the States, Larkin made that memorable appearance in O'Connell Street at one of the Imperial Hotel windows disguised as a priest. My father came home in great spirits after this event. He had looked upon him as a greater man than Connolly. It was my mother who told me of these events.

After the Big Strike the Citizen Army was formed, but the next big event was, of course, the Great War. It is estimated

Old Church Street before being demolished in 1914.

A PROCLAMATION

WHEREAS it has been represented to me, being a Justice of the Peace in and for the County of the City of Dublin by an information duly sworn, that a number of persons will meet or assemble at

SACKVILLE STREET
OR ITS NEIGHBOURHOOD
in the said County of the City of Dublin, on or about
the 31st day of AUGUST, 1913

and that the object of such Meeting or Assemblage is seditious, and that the said Meeting or Assemblage would cause terror and alarm to, and dissension between, His Majesty's subjects, and would be an unlawful assembly.

NOW I do hereby prohibit such Meeting or Assemblage, and do strictly caution and forewarn all Persons whomsoever that they do abstain from taking part in or encouraging or inciting to the same.

AND I do hereby give notice that if in defiance of this Proclamation any such Meeting or Assemblage at Sackville Street or its neighbourhood shall be attempted or take place, the same will be prevented and all Persons attempting to take part in or encouraging the same, or inciting thereto, will be proceeded against according to law.

AND I do hereby enjoin all Magistrates and Officers intrusted with the preservation of the Public Peace, and all others whom it may concern, to aid and assist in the due and proper execution of the Law in preventing any such Meeting or Assemblage as aforesaid, and in the effectual dispersion and suppression of the same, and in the detection and prosecution of those who after this Notice, shall offend in the respects aforesaid.

Given under my hand this 29th day of August, 1913.

E. G. SWIFTE,
Chief Divisional Magistrate, Dublin Metropolitan Police District.

GOD SAVE THE KING.

DUBLIN PRINTED FOR HIS MAJESTY'S STATIONERY OFFICE BY ALEX. THOM & CO., LIMITED ABBEY STREET.

Workers waiting for Larkin's food ship.

that 300,000 Irishmen fought in that First World War. When John Redmond spoke on behalf of conscription in Ireland, my father, who had always followed Redmond, turned completely against him. A number of young men from our district joined the British Army.

I know that Uncle Pat Corcoran, my mother's brother, and my father both joined the Volunteers at the big meeting in the Rotunda in November 1913. Uncle Pat was a compositor, and a great personal friend of Arthur Griffith for and with whom, he had often done some printing jobs.

Three years later as Easter drew near, notices concerning manoeuvres often appeared in the public press. On the Thursday before Easter Sunday a notice appeared in the papers ordering the Volunteers to mobilise for manoeuvres. This was a cover-up for a Rising, but Commander-in-Chief Eoin MacNeill had not been informed of the fact. When he learnt the truth, and was told that arms were arriving from Germany, he was furious. Next, when he heard the bad news that the arms had not arrived, he determined to stop the Rising. He put a notice in the newspapers cancelling the so-called manoeuvres. However, as the world knows, Connolly and Pearse decided to go on, and so at 12 noon on Easter Monday the 1916 Rising began, with only a fraction of the Volunteers taking part.

From what I heard, all of Dublin were surprised when the shooting commenced. Easter Monday was a holiday for everyone and many people had made plans for the day. The Rising put paid to most plans. On Easter Tuesday the British Army made its appearance in our area by taking over Bourkes, the undertakers, in Queen Street.

On the Monday itself the Irish Volunteers had mobilised in the Colmcille Hall in Blackhall Place. Fierce fighting broke out nearby in Church Street and Four Courts area; it has been said that some of the fiercest fighting of the Rising took place here. Ned Daly commanded the Volunteers while just across Queen Street Bridge the Mendicity Institution was taken over by Sean Heuston.

Barricades were erected at the North Dublin Union, Constitution Hill, North King Street and North Brunswick Street. There was a great deal of shooting on the quays, where there were many casualties. Commandant Daly made the Father Matthew Hall his headquarters, and it was used also as a first-aid post by members of Cumann na mBan, that is, the Women's Company. Snipers were settled in the Brunswick Street area, and continuous fire was directed on the Broadstone Station, which the British had taken over. The British had taken over Bourkes the undertakers in Queen Street on Tuesday in the hope of dislodging a sniper perched on the tall Jameson chimney in Smithfield.

The new Bridewell was taken by the Volunteers. Some British soldiers who had moved into Linenhall Barracks surrendered during the week and were made prisoners. The barracks were set on fire. Reilly's Fort at the junction of Church Street and North King Street bore the brunt of much of the fighting. The Blanchardstown Mills on the opposite corner also took a hammering.

My mother told us for years afterwards about the non-stop firing from Church Street, which was only about three hundred yards away. Many civilians were killed in the fighting, some of them by the British soldiers as they searched houses in North King Street.

When it was all over the executions began, and gradually the people woke up to what had been attempted. In 1917, all the prisoners who had been held in England came back to Ireland, and as my father said 'The whole world and Garret Reilly' went out to Kingstown (Dun Laoire) to meet and greet them. From this point on the spirit of nationalism, which had been dormant for so long, began to awaken in the hearts of the Irish people. This feeling grew into an anti-British bias, and was responsible during the next few years for many men 'on the run' being able to elude the military.

The apparently unsuccessful rising was really the first round in the struggle for independence. Sinn Féin prospered from the long delay in implementing Home Rule, and con-scription, or rather the threat of it, clinched it for them. They swept the polls in 1918 and on the wall of our house there appeared a white painted slogan, which remained for years. It was there when we left in 1930, 'To-day is Ireland's day — Vote for Staines'. My mother was disgusted with the slogan, because it disfigured the wall. The ideas of Arthur Griffith, first expounded in 1905, had now surfaced as a do-it-yourself system.

Reilly's Fort.

The Linen Hall after the Rising.

In answer to British force, hostility to the police had spread to every county and many members left the force. It now became a war of guerilla tactics at its best and worst. The next two years were two very important ones.

Every day there was trouble somewhere in town. There were many baton charges by the police and rifle fire was heard often. One Sunday on our way to Aunt Minnie's, there was shooting in Parnell Street near Summerhill. We scrambled out of the No. 23 tram and huddled in the doorway of a tenement house. There was a baton charge just then and we saw crowds of people running towards the Parnell Monument, followed by the police. We had to stay in the hall of the tenement house for over an hour.

The Black and Tans made their first appearance in Dublin in March 1920 and the Auxiliaries — the Auxies — came in July. From this time on the military searches were a daily feature. A street was cordoned off and everyone caught in the net was searched. Sometimes they threw one or two into the lorry and took them away. At first the soldiers went around in open lorries but when the I.R.A. began to drop grenades on them from open windows, it was decided to put cages on the Crosley tenders. As they looked like monkey-cages, we children used make monkey signs at them, scratching under arms and picking imaginery fleas. The Auxies were supposed to consist of ex-army officers.

Curfew was a bad time for my father as very often he was called out on night-work. The D.U.T. Co. got him a pass, but I know now that my mother must have passed many a sleepless night. On two occasions he was picked up, but was brought home in the morning by the military.

1920 was the year of Kevin Barry and Terence MacSwiney. In 1919 Éamon de Valera had escaped from Lincoln Jail and the hunger strikers in Mountjoy had been released, but the pace began to quicken in the year 1920. Many say that from July to September was the worst part of that year. There was trouble in November also, when a Union Jack was flown over the Bank of Ireland in College Green. And all during these times Michael Collins was cycling around on his creaky bicycle with a reward of £10,000 on his head. 'That Michael Collins is a darlin' man, a darlin' man.'

November 1920 also saw Bloody Sunday, when, after the

killing of marked British officers, the army took its revenge in Croke Park. My Uncle Pat who went to the match gave my parents a first hand account of what happened. And in the streets we, the children, were singing loudly 'And we'll crown de Valera King of Ireland'.

There was no easing-up on the fighting as 1921 approached. Two Irishmen were murdered by the Auxies in Drumcondra in February, and in March six Volunteers were hanged in Mountjoy. Nearly every day soldiers and police were being ambushed somewhere in Ireland; while in Dublin there were many skirmishes between Auxies and the Volunteers. A Mr. Carroll was shot at his own door after opening it to the Black and Tans. This happened in Stoneybatter and another local man named Christy Breslin was taken out and shot at Cabra Cross.

While all of this was going on we, the children, lashed our tops, rolled our hoops and played our games. We ran when we heard shooting of course and we shouted 'Up the Rebels' when the lorries passed, but our minds were on the serious business of childhood. We listened to our parents and their friends as they discussed the Trouble, but 'hop and cock a rooshy' always took first place. However, the burning of the Custom House in May caught everybody's attention. Then, suddenly, in the middle of our Summer holidays in 1921 everybody began to use a word which I had never heard before — the word Truce. Up to the coming of the magic word 'Truce', people talked only of raids, shootings, ambushes, reprisals, hunger strikes, curfews and the future was a long dark corridor. The Volunteers, who were only part-time soldiers, could not hope to beat the power of Britain; their object was to make British rule in Ireland impossible. The guerilla tactics succeeded in this and the British Government had to come to terms or else undertake a full-scale military conquest.

The truce was negotiated in July 1921 and eventually, in December, a treaty was signed. In January 1922, all the boys and girls of Oxmantown Green cheered and jeered the British soldiers as they marched down the quays for the last time. Many of the 'oul' wans' of the area were in tears. The band played 'Tipperary' and 'Pack up your Troubles' and the soldiers sang. The boats were waiting for them at the North

Trooper from Marlboro' Barracks in Hanlon's Pub in 1915.

Wall. We had a huge bonfire in Smithfield that night.

The first thing that I noticed was that curfew was no more. We were allowed stay out on the streets in spite of the wintry weather; this was done, I expect, to show how free we were. The fear of shootings and soldiers was gone; but then the grown-ups began to argue again. Very soon we were to learn that there was more trouble and excitement around the corner.

The year 1922 was the most exciting in our district. Around Easter, on a fine sunny morning, we woke up to find Smithfield and the Haymarket filled with men drilling. We did not know it at the time, but this was the start of the Civil War. A few of them, those shouting the orders, had uniforms; the others had bandoliers and belts and rifles. We, as children always do, were running in and out among them, but they didn't seem to mind. My father had gone to work and didn't hear about it until that evening. By that time, they had left Smithfield and taken over the Four Courts.

Everybody expected trouble straight away, but nothing happened. The men were in the Four Courts for over two months, and sometimes after school we went down to talk to some of them, as they were arranging barbed wire along the inside of the railings and piling sandbags near the gates.

'Hey, mister, what are yez doin'?'

'We're tryin' to keep the Free Staters out.'

'Outa where, mister?'

'If you don't run off home now, I'll tan your little arse for you.'

We had just got our holidays in June from Brunner when it started. Lorries began to arrive in Smithfield and the place was full of soldiers in green uniforms. I have a faint recollection of some wearing khaki uniforms and some 'oul' wans' shouting 'The Tommies are back!' The shooting commenced immediately, most of the gunfire from the Four Courts, coming from the big dome. All the boys and girls came out to watch, and some of us were quite close to what *we* called the fifty-six pounders in Phoenix Street, as they were fired. The soldiers made attempts to chase us away, even threatening to shoot us. We just stood there and held our ears as the big guns went off. However, a military order was given to all parents to keep their children indoors. From that on, I watched the firing out of the Four Courts dome from our bedroom window. Actually, it was a grandstand view and no one seemed to worry about flying bullets. The window we used was the one that looked out on Bridewell Lane. The rattle of gunfire was very clear, and we could see the puffs coming out of the dome. It was all very exciting.

'Them fellas must be mad. What are they tryin' to do? Get us all killed?'

'Them's de Valera's men. He says the Treaty is a bad one and shouldn't ha' been signed ar' all.'

'Yeh, but what are they doin' in the Four Courts? Why don't they attack the Royal Barracks?'

'There aren't enough of them. But isn't it bloody awful? Some of them fellas are fightin' against their own brothers.'

'I wisht they'd make up their twittin' minds. I was on me way down to Heathers on Arran Quay to buy a pillow-slip, when a bloody big bogman of a soldier let a roar at me. I nearly foaled a fiddle with the fright.'

'I don't think them Irregulars will last long in the Four Courts. Sure they'll be short of grub and ammunition very soon.'

'Well, the way I see it, it's really a war now between Michael Collins and de Valera. Why can't they shake hands and be friends? Haven't we had our bellyful of war?'

For two whole days the one sentence that was used over and over was 'They're firing out of the dome still'. The Free State soldiers were billeted on the local people. One of the officers shouted up to us to open up and then went to the door of the Woods family next door. They didn't realise that our front door was around the corner. My mother and father were glad to escape this meal-serving business. Their feelings towards Free Staters were rather luke-warm. The two of them loved Michael Collins, but there was always a graw in their hearts for Éamon de Valera. It was difficult to take sides.

As the end drew near, we watched the dome, as it went up in flames. The huge copper top seemed to rise up on one side and then topple over. After the surrender, the prisoners were brought to Smithfield, to Jamesons. As they lined up behind iron bars, one of the prisoners, Rory O'Connor they said, bent one bar and six or seven prisoners ran out among the huge crowd that had gathered. Immediately, the soldiers commenced to fire over the heads of everybody, but we thought they were firing at us. The stampede was frightening. I tore across Smithfield, across Haymarket and down Burgess Lane. Pulling the string, which was always left in our letter-box, I opened the door. No sooner was the front door opened, than a wave of humanity carried me in. The crowd filled the bedrooms upstairs, the stairway, the kitchen and the parlour — even the yard was jammed. I could hear four Rosaries being recited at the same time — one in each room. After about an hour the people began to leave in twos and threes, and soon we, the family, were left on our own. My mother checked every room immediately and informed us that not a thing had been taken. Honesty was a way of life then.

The gang and myself were sad to see it all over. It had been a time of great excitement; I had been sent on messages during the shooting. It was safe to move westwards away from Smithfield. After the surrender, we went around picking up empty rifle cartridges. These we brought to school after the summer holidays to use as pencil holders. We swapped them also for other items like marbles or pens. The other boys were jealous that we had seen it all.

After the surrender of the Four Courts, fighting broke out in many city areas and the well-known Cathal Brugha was the first major casualty. I had seen pictures of him in the paper and I remember saying to myself, as Mossy and I moved around his coffin in the Mater Hospital, 'He looks the very same as his picture'. He was laid out in his uniform.

The fighting lasted almost a year, but it passed over the heads of us children. It was nothing compared with the British occupation. Around the country, the Irregulars, as they were called, found that they were fighting their brothers, who knew the local terrain as well as themselves. Before the Civil War ended, both Griffith and Collins were dead. With my mother, I watched the two funerals — there was a ten day interval between 'them — from the same vantage point, outside Trinity College.

From now on I began to hear new names in the arguments

among grown-ups. The three big names were those of
Cosgrave, O'Higgins and Mulcahy. This now became the time
of executions and by January 1923 over fifty Republicans
had been executed. Twenty-seven more were to die before
the end of the war. At last on May 24, 1923, the Civil War
ended, but not before most of the talented and dedicated
men were dead. 'Take my word for it, oul' son, we were left
with nuttin' but rubbish. The crame was gone.'

*Angle Court off Beresford Street in 1913. The poverty of Dublin under
British rule.*

9 Street Characters

*'Mary Ockey' and 'Mad Essie' — 'Drummer Maher' and '
Pound Note' — 'Mullinahack' — 'Slep' with the Nuns' —
'Daddy Egan' — 'Hairy Lemon' and 'Toucher Doyle' — The
Lavender Man and 'Bah!' — The Barrel-organ man — 'Bang
Bang' on the trams — 'Penny's the Song' and 'Johnny Forty
Coats' — Weep! Weep! — Rags, bones and bottles — 'Corny
Neill', the King.*

AS IN OTHER Dublin districts characters abounded in ours.
Mary Ockey and Mad Essie were the only two female
characters that I remember except, of course, the little old
lady with the flat straw hat and shawl who seemed to know
only one song. This song she sang outside of Keogh's and
Minogue's at the corner of Benburb Street and St. John's,
the pub at the corner of Haymarket, every Friday. The song
was 'Mick McGilligan's Daughter, Mary Ann'; so that is what
she was called. Years later, I found out that her name was
Crosbie.

Other characters were Drummer Maher and Pound Note.
Pound Note derived his name from the story that he once
found a pound note, and ever after, would never pass a piece
of paper on the ground. He was easily recognisable from his
bulging clothes, the pockets and linings of which were
packed with paper of all kinds.

Most characters were of the toucher, begging type, but one
who was not, was 'Slep' with the Nuns'. I don't know how
the poor man got his name, but that is the name which we
called after him. He ranged the Stoneybatter area and seemed
to come from Blackhorse Lane. When called by this name, he
stood out in the middle of the road and let loose a string of
curses, the likes of which I never heard before or since.

There was another middle-aged man, who begged from

door to door. We called him Mullinahack, because whenever he was given a penny, or a ha'penny, he smiled and said 'They'll never bate the Chinese out of Mullinahack'. He always wore a flat, peaked cap and white runner shoes. Calling him Mullinahack made no impression on him; he simply smiled and went his way.

My father had a name for a cornet player, who played every Sunday outside the pubs. The tune was 'Happy Moments', and that is what my father called him. The music always sounded so sad, and on a wet Sunday, it sounded even sadder.

Then there was Daddy Egan, who owned a pub at the north end of Smithfield, facing Bergin's farm-produce shop. He was a grey-haired old man who stopped children on the street to give each a prayer leaflet plus a penny to light a candle. I am afraid that most of us spent the money on sweets. Hairy Lemon was another raggedy character, who always had dogs with him, but one of the best known and liked in the area was Toucher Doyle, who lived in Hendrick Street. How he managed it no one knows, but he mixed with the 'nobs' of the so-called aristocracy of the time at race-meetings and other functions. He was to be found in the front line in pictures of every big event, and after a successful day at a race-meeting always called for drinks for everybody in St. John's pub in Queen Street.

There was also the Lavender Man down town, whose territory ranged from Grafton Street to the G.P.O. One particular character who amused me — we had no name for him — was a peaked-capped, sick-looking man of about thirty-five, who sketched on the pavement on O'Connell Bridge. In the evenings, he walked both sides of O'Connell Street, and when coming face to face with two or three girls, he suddenly threw out his hands, jumped in front of them letting a very, very loud BAH! from his lips. The girls got a terrible fright, of course, but our friend continued on his way laughing, and ready to frighten the next group. I forgot to mention that he had a startlingly red nose.

Every Wednesday at about 5 o'clock, a man trundled his barrel-organ into the Haymarket, followed by his wife, a very thin woman. He parked the organ outside Scanlan's, the saddler, and straightaway commenced to turn the handle.

The tunes were ones we had heard often like 'Nellie Dean', 'Peggy O'Neill', 'Sweet Rosie O'Grady' and so on. The girls and the very small children danced on the path and on the roadway. At this time of day, that is 5 p.m., most of the carts had disappeared. 'Hey, mister, me mudder wants to know will you play Danny Boy.' Grown-ups stood at doors or watched from windows. The man's wife stood on the pathway and held out a cloth bag. Mrs. Cullen always sent out a child with a penny, and the wife went around to some of the doors and knocked. Neither the man nor his wife ever said anything; they came in silence and went away in silence. From the Haymarket, they always went to Minogue's pub at the corner of Benburb Street, and of course all of the children followed them. The dancing by the girls continued there, and then at about half past five the man would suddenly shut the side of the organ, take up the shafts and pull away the barrel-organ, followed by his wife.

Nicknames from the Church Street and Anne Street area reached our ears from time to time. I heard of Bah Furlong, Chase the Hearse, the Bare Wall, Red Pole Welsh, Chucky Hayes and Tall Hayes and the Yank Mooney.

Bang! Bang! appeared on our scene in the Twenties, but he belonged to the entire city. His favourite hunting-ground was the trams, from one of which he jumped, turning immediately to fire 'Bang Bang' at the conductor. Passengers and passers-by took up the game, and soon an entire street of grown-ups were shooting at each other from doorways and from behind lamp-posts. The magic of make-believe childhood took over, and it was all due to the simple innocence of 'Bang Bang'. He was a very young man at this time. 'Bang! You're shot. If yeh don't die, I'm not playin'.' My father was very fond of him, and seemed to come across him very often in different parts of the city. He told us about one incident with 'Bang Bang' in Marlboro' Street, where the shooting pretence went on for nearly half-an-hour and some visiting Americans joined in. They thought the whole thing hilarious.

The following is the text of an *Irish Independent* item on 'Bang Bang' at the time of his death on 12th January 1981: 'One of Dublin's best known and most beloved characters Tommy 'Bang Bang' Dudley has died in a home for the blind.

He was 75.

He was an institution in Dublin during his lifetime. He carried a huge jail key with him around the city, mockingly pointing it at strangers and shouting 'Bang Bang'.

Despite progressive eye disease, 'Bang Bang' maintained his daily beat in the city frequently causing mayhem by jumping onto buses, slapping his rear end as if he was on a horse.

Only recently he told his friends on his sickbed in Clonturk House for the Adult Blind in Drumcondra, Dublin, that he got the idea for his 'Bang Bang' characterisations from the many cowboy films that he attended in his early years. He lived in various parts of the city during his lifetime — in Mill Lane for 41 years and later in Bridgefoot Street flats.

Full funeral arrangements will be made today.'

In the Stoneybatter area, there was 'Boo Paw', who sold boot polish from door to door. He got his name from his street-call. At a later stage down-town there were 'Penny's the Song' and 'Johnny Forty Coats'. These two characters belonged to all of Dublin. 'Penny's the Song' sold popular songs printed on small sheets; he was still there in the 1950s. Everybody knew 'Johnny Forty Coats'.

On Thursdays, a huge woman came from the direction of Benburb Street striding along Bridewell Lane and in a fog-horn voice, let everyone know that she had 'Fish, fresh fish! Dublin Bay herrin's and whitenin'.' I never saw her with a barrow; she carried a huge basket on her head and wore a black shawl, of course. Her white apron was spotless and she was the picture of health itself. We had a cockle-woman also who came on no special day and there was 'Weep Weep'. He was the sweep, of course, and children were afraid of him on account of his black face. It seemed strange that even in the early morning, when starting on his rounds, his face was black.

The tinkers came often. These were tinsmiths and within five minutes would have your leaking kettle or pot mended. I think the arrival of plastic put an end to the tinker's trade. However some of the tinkers switched over to mending broken umbrellas. In the Twenties, they didn't beg.

Rag and bone men or balloon men were quite numerous.

They came through the Haymarket with their barrows of balloons and windmills shouting 'Any rags, bones or bottles!'. For old shirts or blouses one got a balloon. I could never make out how the word 'bones' got into their street-cry. We all made a bee-line for our homes as soon as we heard their cry. Balloons had a great appeal. One other character we all remember was Johnny Rea (Ray), an Italian, who sold his own ice-cream from his own barrow. He had a place in Smithfield at first, where he made his ice-cream, which he sold in wafers and cones at a penny and a ha'penny. He moved later up to Thomas Street, near Cornmarket.

Finally at the King Street end of Queen Street, there lived a huge man named Corny Neill. He was a jarvey, and one evening there was great jubilation in Queen Street, when Corny was crowned King of the Jarveys. As far as I know this was an All-Dublin title. I think everybody knows the song of the Dublin jarvey:

'If you want to drive round Dublin
Sure you'll find me on the stand;
I'll take you to Raheny
For cockles on the strand,
To Phoenix Park, to Nancy Hands,
The Monument and then
I'll take you to the Strawberry Beds
And back to town again.'

The world seemed full of jaunting cars and the horse was king of the roads and streets. The world was still rosy.

All of these characters were ever-present during my boyhood. Some of the names given to them were unkind, to say the least, but the bearers of these colourful names meant so much to life on the Dublin streets. Our Dublin would not have been the same without them.

There were other characters who had no nicknames and I can remember the story of the two oul' wans from Hendrick Street, who found themselves in court one day:

'Now Mrs. Murphy, tell the court what happened.'

'There I was fixin' me washin' on the small line on the landin'. I was up on a chair, so I was, and who should come up the stairs but your gills, Mrs. Byrne. And what does she do, but lifts me skirt and me on the chair, and bites me in the arse. (laughter) I filled a basin with the blood so I did, a whole basin.'

'She's a bloody liar, your warship. How could I bite anyone? Sure I haven't a tooth in me head, look!' (laughter)

'Don't believe that barren oul' bitch. Search her, she has the two sets in her pocket. (laughter) Unless she left them in the Pawn. (laughter). And then she ran off. Would an innocent woman do that? The polisman found her hidin' in Mr. Moore's back passage.' (Judge fell off his seat here).

Tenements in Nth. King Street (taken from Queen Street), known locally as The Cherry Steps.

10 Boyish Pranks and Escapades

Ganseys and short trousers — 'Skull' caps and shawls — 'Maggie wants the Po Po!' — Down in the Liffey — Tony Mangan missing — Tying the knockers — Running through the pubs — Wilson the Rilson — Battling Siki in Haymarket — The Smithfield Gang — Climbing the roofs — Stone-throwing wars — Bulldog McKeown.

THE COMMON KIND of apparel for boys in the early Twenties was the gansey and short trousers. Before that, during the War years, many boys wore a kind of suit with knickerbockers, that is, trousers which buttoned at the knees to meet the stockings. The short trousers of the Twenties were worn by all boys and getting into 'longers' signified that a lad had reached the first step to adulthood. The word teenager hadn't been invented and very little attention was paid to boys and girls of that age. There was very little or no vandalism and the term juvenile delinquent had yet to be concocted.

Large white bibs were all the fashion among young girls. Many girls, big and small, wore hats and, of course, no lady would enter a church with head uncovered.

I wore a school or skull cap like many others. All the men and youths wore soft caps with peaks. Anyone wearing a trilby or soft hat had to be 'posh'. In summer, straw hats appeared and children in Dublin played a game with a rhyme:

'I see a straw baymer one, two, three,
No body has it only me.'

Then the rhymer ran and tipped the straw hat on the owner's head, sometimes knocking it off.

Shawls, black ones, were always worn by the Dublin hawkers and, indeed, many women who were not hawkers wore them also. Now and again we noticed women with

Rags and an old Dublin barrow.

brownish, patterned shawls. The hawkers going to and coming from the market pushed a wicker-like barrow. This had three iron wheels, the odd wheel being at the front. They were of good depth and must have been identical with the one referred to in the song:

'And she wheeled her wheelbarrow,
Through streets broad and narrow,
Crying Cockles and Mussels
Alive, Alive - O.'

The women sold their wares from the barrows.

Some of the women who did not wear shawls looked down on those who did, like the woman in Mangan's poem *Woman of Three Cows*, where the woman who possessed three cows looked down on the woman who had only two. In wet weather, the shawl was put up over the head. Some shawled women wore hats; they were always the same model, a plain straw-hat, with a pill-box shape. Large pins were stuck through them, to keep them on. They were all Biddy Mulligans in the Twenties.

When my playmates and myself were very young we watched oul' wans in shawls coming out of pubs and pretending to stand to talk to each other over the railings that led down to the cellars of the pub, while urinating openly down into the cellar. It was too good to be missed by mischievous children, so we chanted, 'Maggie wants the Po Po; Maggie wants the Po Po'. This always enraged them so much that, along with a string of curses, we were called brats, cnats, sleeveens, bastards, corner boys and many other names.

Later on, I understood the predicament of these women. A ladies' toilet in a pub was an unheard-of item; in fact the women usually disappeared into the snug. In my own estimation the number of drinking women at this time was not very big. There was always sawdust on the floor of the pub and three or four spitoons for the men, and respectable women would never be seen entering a public house. Any woman who did go in had to be prepared for discomfort.

At the ripe age of seven I was playing one day at the horse trough with Tony, Kevin, Philip and Paddy when a suggestion came from Tony:

'I know where we can catch crabs!'

'You don't!' (in ordinary conversation — You're a liar
   You're another liar)
'You're another, I do.' (You're another liar)
'I'm not goin' out to Merrion; me mother wouldn't let
   me.'
'Yez don't have to go to Merrion; come on and I'll
   show you.'
Tony led the way. He brought us down Queen Street past his
father's barber's shop and across the road on Arran Quay. He
got over the wall and started to go down the steps to the
Liffey.
   'We're not goin' down there; a Rozzer'll chase us.'
   'All right, I'm goin' meself.'
We watched as he reached the bottom. The tide was out and
Tony started to walk around on the stones, lifting one here
and there.
   We looked at one another. It seemed alright and besides,
we might get some crabs. Down the steps we went, one after
another. Some oul' fella shouted at us to 'come up owa
that'. In a few minutes we were walking around the Liffey-
bed picking up or turning up stones. We were there for a
long time and still no sign of a crab. There were bicycle
frames and bedsteads and plenty of bottles, but no crabs.
And just then there was a shout from Tony. We rushed over
to him slipping on the slimy stones.
   'Let's see it, let's see the crab.'
   'It's not a crab; but look what I found.'
It was a very large silver coin. We found out afterwards that it
was a Queen Victoria Crown worth five shillings. We forgot
about the crabs and commenced to look for money.
   It was then I noticed a man waving to us from the top of a
24 Tram coming along the quays. It was my father. When I
got home later my mother was waiting for me. It was she
who looked after the discipline in our home, as my father
was rather soft-hearted. She had a thin leather thong, which
she used mercilessly on our legs. I can tell you we were
obedient and respectful children. My mother, of course, was
no different to the other mothers of that period. If a boy
came home with the news that he had been walloped in
school, he received a second helping at home.

Bridge and Liffey at Queen Street.

There was consternation around the Haymarket in the Autumn of 1919 when it was discovered that Tony Mangan was missing. Everybody went searching; there wasn't a hiding place that wasn't visited. Even the roofs were searched, the Big Yard in Smithfield, the interiors of the weigh-houses, the greenhouses, the shops, the aytin' houses, every place, even the confessionals in Arran Quay and in Church Street. For the first time the picture show in the 'Feeno' was interrupted and a notice read out to the audience. Darkness had fallen and all the neighbours were trying to console Mrs. Mangan, when a 'phone call was received at the Bridewell. A D.M.P. man came with the message to poor Mrs. Mangan: Tony was in Mulhuddart, County Dublin. He had fallen asleep on a pile of hay, which had been left on one of the haycarts. The farmer didn't notice him in the hay; so he hitched up and left. At Mulhuddart Tony woke up. He arrived home in a motor-car and got a hero's welcome. The whole thing was a nine days' wonder. All of which showed the simplicity of Dublin people's lives at the beginning of the second decade. We were jealous of him.

'What did the oul' fella say to yeh, Tony?'

'He said nuttin'; he gave me a shillin'.'

'He didn't?'

'You're another, he did — look.'

He showed us the shilling, but we still didn't believe him.

'I bet he bet the lard owa yeh?'

'He didn't, he did give me a shillin'. May I be stiffened, if I'm tellin' a lie.'

'Show us your teeth!'

'Look, there's no black on me teeth. Now, amn't I tellin' the truth?'

'Well, what happened anyway?'

'When I woke up I started bawlin' and the oul' fella didn't know where I kem from. I told him I wanted to go home to Queen Street. So he knocked at a cottage in Mulhuddart.'

'Where's Mulhuddart?'

'It's miles down the country; the people were real country.'

'Who owned the car you kem back in?'

'I don't know; me mudder said he was a Protestant.'

There was a knock on our door one sunny morning; outside were four of the gang: 'Come on the tar is comin' up on the road.' This always happened during a heat wave. The tar used to come up in bubbles between the stone setts on the roadway. We went around pressing the bubbles with our thumbs; this caused water to squirt upwards and was a source of tremendous enjoyment to us. The bigger the bubble of tar, the bigger the squirt of water. On arriving home the questions began:

'Were you playin' with tar again?'

'We were only burstin' the bubbles.'

'I'll burst your head for you; look at your hands! How are we goin' to get that tar off?'

'Tony says you can get it off with butter?'

'Does Tony Mangan know the price of butter?'

The butter always did the trick. It softened the tar and made it easier to wash off.

There was an engineering shop at No. 58 Smithfield next door to Head's the blacksmith. There was a lot to be seen from the big open gate and a crowd of us often gathered to watch the wheels and belts going round and round. Mr. Wilson had three men working for him. However, he didn't like the idea of spectators at his door, so he used make a run at us. We kept coming back and this annoyed him so much that he chased one or two around to their homes, where he complained to the parents. One time, when he chased me, instead of running home I headed up Smithfield and got away. Mr. Wilson wore a black oily cap and had a moustache. Our last encounter with him was when about six of us stood at his gate and sang 'Wilson, the Rilson, the Rick Stick, Stilson'.

This was a chant to suit every name e.g. 'Murphy, the Burphy, the Rick Stick Surphy', or 'Mangan, the Langan, the Rick Stick Stangan'. Then out of nowhere came a policeman, or polisman, as he was called. He grabbed Michael Lyons and myself and took our names and addresses. After that, we never annoyed Mr. Wilson again, although we never heard from the law.

We played the old trick which was in common use everywhere, that is, tying a black thread to a knocker and hiding in another doorway or around the corner. Other times, we tied two knockers together with black thread and watched the results. However, the real excitement for us youngsters lay in a chase. For real thrills we ran through one door of a pub and out through another. Sometimes a barman waited and one or other of us was sent bawling from a clout of a wet cloth. Our favourite haunts were St. John's pub in Haymarket and Baker's Hall on the quay. There was a back entrance to Baker's Hall from Coke Lane and it was very exciting to run right through and out onto Arran Quay. I shall never forget the day I ran full tilt into a fat man carrying two pints. My father had to pay for them.

One day, there was a great commotion in Haymarket. Philip Fitzsimons knocked at our door and shouted, 'Come on quick, there's a black man throwing away money'. Up to the Haymarket with the two of us; there up on a hackney car was the first blackman I ever saw in the flesh. We had seen blackmen in the pictures, but there were none in Dublin as far as I knew. He was 'Grushying' money in the shape of sixpences, threepenny bits, pennies, ha'pennies and farthings. He seemed to have his pockets full of them. As we joined the crowds of children — there must have been a couple of hundred and I could see Mossy in the thick of them, he threw another handful. I was lucky enough to catch a threepenny bit in mid-air. Just then, the horse took fright at all the commotion and began to gallop. The last we saw of the blackman was his waving back at us, as the hackney careered towards New Church Street. His name was Battling Siki and he was due to fight Mike McTigue in the La Scala Cinema the next day for the Light Heavyweight Championship of the World. Looking back now I remember him as being very ugly; he was wearing a light grey suit. Regarding the threepenny bit, I dashed over to Mrs. Cullen's shop with the others — everybody seemed to have got something — and the old lady did a roaring business for about an hour. Bottles of Vimto and penny buns were the items most sought after. Vimto tasted like the present-day Cola.

That night, when my father came in with the paper, there on the front page was a picture of the two boxers. He wouldn't believe that we actually met Battling Siki and as neither Mossy nor myself could produce the money that we had got, his disbelief remained. The next day, he heard the story from other sources and only then did he realise that it wasn't our imagination.

Soon enough I began to make new friends. You could say that the Haymarket gang joined with the Smithfield gang. These boys lived at the south end of Smithfield itself and their names were Frank and Mick Fogarty, grandsons of old Mrs. Fogarty in the Haymarket, Philip Furlong, Richie and Arthur Corr, Ginchy Roche and Patsy Devine. This was the time when both groups developed a craze for climbing. We climbed the roofs of the weigh-houses, we climbed to the top of Jameson's wall and ran along the ledge, we climbed onto the roof of Doyle the coachbuilder (when the workers had gone), we climbed over the wall next to the Cork Dairy in Queen Street, where there was a derelict site. Tony Mangan was able to reach this place from a side window in his own house.

We climbed and played also in the Big Yard, as the Fogartys called it, which was at the rear of the house, where the Fogartys lived. Climbing walls and houses was an unusual form of playing I suppose, but status in the gang depended on one's ability to do such things. However, something else happened which was caused by the amalgamation of Haymarket and Smithfield.

Nearby was the Hentown gang, the name deriving from the name Hendrick Street. A war (?) commenced between the two areas, a war which was waged with stones as ammunition. The stone-throwing commenced after tea and continued until darkness fell. There were frequent sallies and retreats interspersed by shouts from women at doors or windows. 'If yez don't stop that stone-throwing I'll send for the pólis.' The war lasted a couple of weeks and then fizzled out. At a later time a war on a larger scale developed between the Church Street and Mary's Lane gang and the combined strength of Hentown, Smithfield and Haymarket. This war also faded out. The battle-field was Smithfield, 'Yez snotty-nosed little cnats; I'll be dug outa yez.' It was about this time that I became friendly with two other boys, older than myself. Their names were Bunny Carter and Pimple Kavanagh

Robert Emmet's house, No. 4 Haymarket.

and they lived in Phoenix Street. Bunny used to get free passes for the 'Feeno' and brought me with him quite often. This was my first taste of luxury at a picture, as the free pass entitled us to two seats in the 'cushioners'. I think Bunny and Pimple attended the boys' school in Queen Street, Dicky Piersse's.

Another late arrival in our gang was Brendan McKeown. He was christened Bulldog and lived in Robert Emmet's house in Haymarket. Brendan differed from the rest of us, because his people were rather well-off. His father was partner in the then well-known 'McKeown and McKeogh, auctioneers, valuers, hay and corn factors'. Their house was a three storey over basement, Georgian-type building and Tony, Kevin, Philip and the rest of us were afraid to go into the basement. The reason for this was the presence of a man-servant, who was deaf and dumb. We called him the Dummy in the cruel way of children, and used run when we saw him coming. One day, I met him on the stairs. 'Is Brendan in?' I asked him. 'Uh! Uh!' he answered. He was wearing his peaked cap, which he never took off. 'Is Brendan in?' I asked again. 'Uh! Uh!' he answered again and came down towards me. I took to my heels. Anyway, we all kept clear of the deaf mute. I think he was the cook in the basement kitchen.

Brendan laughed at us, of course. He was a burly, well-built boy, slightly older than myself and attending Belvedere College. One year he won the Leinster Boys' Swimming Championship for the 100 yards, and on account of this, we regarded him with some awe. His swimming prowess placed him in a higher category than the rest of the group.

The McKeowns had a new Model T Ford plus a chauffeur, Mr. Handley. He used to chase us for blowing the horn on the car. On occasions, Brendan brought us into his backyard, which was really a farmyard with hens, stables and sheds. The mixed smell of hay, horse-piss and potatoes was quite over-powering. It was in McKeown's hen house in a nest of straw that I saw a freshly-laid egg for the first time in my life. It was unbelievable that a hen had produced such a clean white article.

The McKeowns had three yard-men working for them and had a lorry, a dray and two horses. The man in charge was named Stephen, who didn't like any of the local kids coming

Loading the Guinness fleet of lighters, Victoria Quay 1904. This fleet went out of service in 1931.

into the yard. Although he joined us and played with us sometimes, Bulldog was never really a member of the gang.

Then there were the Guinness barges. The firm had their jetty at Victoria Quay, where the men stacked up the barrels on the barges. I often watched them start their journey to the North Wall. At other times, Tony, Kevin and myself waited at Queen Street Bridge for them. As the fully-laden barge came up to the bridge, one of the men lowered the funnel to allow a safe passage under the centre-arch of the bridge. 'They're off to the Isle o' Man and all those foreign countries.' Then there was a concerted rush by us to the other side to see it come into view again. It was then we set up the cry together, the cry, that had been part and parcel of small boys of Dublin City for generations, 'Hey, mister, bring us back a parrot.'

All of the city was lit by gaslight, and there were many men employed as lamp-lighters. Every one of these was called Billy the Lamplighter. We often followed our local Billy and watched him as he opened the little glass door on the bottom of the lamp frame to turn on the gas. There was one lamp on the corner of our lane, a couple of yards from our door. This lit up our part of the lane at night. There was a Dublin rhyme about Billy the Lamplighter, which I have forgotten.

11 The Phoenix Park

The Mollymount — the gap in the Zoo railings — The band in the Hollow — Polo on Saturday — Cricket — The Magazine River — The Furry Glen and Knockmaroon — Parkgate Street — Minding my young brother — Chestnut time in the Park.

AS WE LIVED near the Phoenix Park it is quite natural to expect that we spent a lot of time there. To us children, the Park was the place where the Wellington Monument, or 'Mollymount' as we pronounced it, was, plus the Gough Statue, the Zoo, the ducks in the Peoples Gardens and the Dog Pond.

The Park was another place we paid sneak visits to, unknown to our parents. Paddy Stynes and Hobby, Tony Mangan, Frank Fogarty and I spent many a happy hour playing on the Wellington Obelisk. We climbed up the sides to touch the figures in the battle scenes. We ran around the top steps and raced down the slanted ones. On other occasions we moved over towards the Conyngham Road wall, beneath the trees, to enjoy the simple pleasurable sight of trains shunting in the Kingsbridge area, and also to experience the thrill of seeing an engine and carriages heading straight towards us only to disappear under the roadway and under our own feet. This was the tunnel that travels under the Park — under the Wellington Monument itself, they said.

In the Peoples Gardens we threw stones at the ducks and were chased by the 'gardener'. In 1921, an English boy named Harry Wicksell, who lived over Eastman's, the butchers, in Queen Street, and who joined our group for the short time that he lived there, informed us that he knew a way into the Zoo that cost no money. It was 3 d. entrance fee at this time. He brought us — there were about ten of us altogether — up to the rear side of the Zoo near the polo grounds, and sure enough, two of the rails were missing. The ten of us made our way in and enjoyed ourselves immensely, much more, probably, than those who had paid. We paid many a visit to see the animals by this means, until 1924 when Paddy Stynes broke the news that the railings had been repaired. I didn't believe him, until I saw it with my own two eyes. Today, there are kangaroos at that particular spot.

Sunday was a great day in the Phoenix Park in the summertime. A band came and played in the Hollow, where the band-stand was situated. Dubliners, most of them from the tenements, came in their hundreds to the Hollow, where Harringtons of the Kiosk had rows and rows of collapsible chairs arranged around the stand. A chair cost 2d. and they always filled up quickly; the remainder of the crowd seated themselves on the tier-like slopes of the Hollow. It was an amphitheatre.

'When me mudder brin's us walkin'
On a Sunday to the Park,
Me father wears his good brown suit,
An' his bowler hat so dark;
Us kids are washed and shinin',
Not a speck o' dirt, or mark,
When me mudder brin's us walkin'
On a Sunday to the Park.

The neighbours watch us leavin'
An' me mudder shoves the pram,
With her head held high in her new straw hat,
An' me father is like a lamb.
Us kids try to hurry,
But me mudder lets a roar,
'Nellie, take young Billy's hand;
Mickser, shut that door'.

The procession moves off slowly;
Mrs. Byrne shouts, 'Where's your whip?'
But me mudder just ignores and sez,
'That Byrne's a right oul' rip'
We pass the corner safely,

Then down along the quay,
Then me mudder says 'Stop scratchin', Joe,
Or all the people'll see'.

Me father buys us cornets,
An' we all commence to lick,
An' me mudder keeps on talkin'
While she aims a clout at Mick.
And so we reach the Park gate,
While she gives out the pay,
An' at last we reach the 'Holla',
Where the band begins to play.

That's the time I love the bestest,
When we all sit on the grass;
She takes the baby on her knee,
And she smiles at all that pass.
She's a different sort of woman,
An' doesn't try to nark,
She just sits there an' listens,
On a Sunday, in the Park.

An' me father smokes there smilin',
An' the sun shines in the sky,
An' we play cowboys thru' the crowd,
An' when we're shot, we die.
The band plays lovely music,
We meet chiselers that we know,
An' the hawkers sell us oranges,
An' we start the skins to throw.

But then the Angelus rings out,
And back we go for bread;
Me mudder an' father are talkin'
To a couple called Betty and Ned.
They're laughin' like mad about sumpin',
That happened, why, long years ago,
We listen, and they keep on talkin',
An' sez me father, 'Remember poor Joe'.

At last, we're collected an' counted,

Lord Gough statue, Phoenix Park.

until the possession of a bicycle made a visit to them possible.

At the Parkgate Street entrance to the Park, there was always a line of hawkers right down to Infirmary Road. It was like a miniature Moore Street on Sundays in Summer, and there was always an ice-cream man in their midst. The hawkers sold fizz drinks at a penny a glass, as well as the usual fruit. The fizz drinks were either pink or plain.

The large, brightly-coloured advertisements on the giant billboards in Parkgate Street never failed to catch the eye of everyone including small boys like myself. The favourites of our gang were the two Bovril ones. One was a picture of a disgustingly healthy-looking man in pyjamas clinging, with one arm, to the neck of a gigantic Bovril bottle, which was floating in the middle of the ocean, with the caption BOVRIL PREVENTS THAT SINKING FEELING. The other hand was held up high in a wave gesture. The second Bovril advertisement depicted a cold snowy country scene, with a small, young bull in aggressive mood, preventing a portly doctor, armed with his black bag, from entering a garden gate, which led to a cottage. This one had the apt title of A LITTLE BOVRIL KEEPS THE DOCTOR AWAY.

I remember also Tinori Corn Cure, Sloan's Liniment and Dr. Cassell's Tablets. Others that lasted a long time were the Kreushen Salts one, and the one for Doan's Backache Kidney Pills. The former showed a healthy-looking man vaulting a gate, while the latter had a picture of a man feeling his sore back. The caption here was 'Every Picture Tells a Story'. The Bisto Kids were there to the fore also. We passed the huge bill-boards in Parkgate Street on our way to the Park every second day in the summertime.

After my younger brother was born in December, 1922 I had a special chore to do on Saturday mornings and also on some afternoons during the school holidays. I had to wheel young Gaby in a go-car up to the Phoenix Park and mind him there. It was a tiresome task but sometimes I persuaded Philip or Tony, or someone else, to come along. My mother thought she was passing her youngest into safe hands, but she would have been shocked to see the things we did with the go-car. I used let it run down the inclined entrance to the Peoples Gardens. I raced ahead and got to the edge of the path leading to Parkgate Street, just in time to meet it and stop it. I also sat on the edge of the go-car with Gaby in the seat, of course, and drove it down the same incline. On other occasions, if one or two of my chums were with me, we took Gaby out, left him on the grass and gave each other jaunts on the cart along the paths, careering along at top speed. One day, on the steep rough path that leads down to the Hollow, one of the wheels broke. We limped home, where I told the truth — the wheel had broken. This was 1924.

October time was chestnut time and the Phoenix Park was the best place in Dublin for them. We went in groups up along the main road. Sometimes we climbed and tried to pick them, but this was not as effective as using a thick piece of wood or a hurley. If thrown, the stick was almost bound to strike some chestnut. I always experienced a feeling of wonder at the pure shiny brownness of the nut, when the outer shell-covering was broken. I often made a bandolier of the chestnuts by stringing about thirty or so on a piece of twine. A hole was punched through the centre of the nut with a nail. In the school-yard one heard:
'How many are you the conqueror of?'
'Twelve!'
'I'm the conqueror of fourteen!'
In a case like this the winner of the above tussle became the conqueror of twenty-six. Chestnuts often fell on the school-room floor, and of course, they were confiscated or thrown into the bin. The chestnut season lasted for the month of October.

Nowadays, one hears the expression — it must have come from America — of 'chasing women'. Such a phrase was unknown to the young Dubliners of forty and fifty years ago. They were, of course, chasing women, but the Dublin phrase was more picturesque — 'clickin' mots'. The favourite place for 'clickin' mots' was the main road of the Phoenix Park.
'Hey, young fellas! Here's young wans.'
'Am I goin'?'
'Yes, in the knees.' (nee-ez)
When a boy or girl became friendly, they commenced to 'do a line'. He became her 'fella' and she became his 'mot'. A

rushed marriage was referred to as a 'military wedding'.

Before I leave the subject of the Phoenix Park in the Twenties, I feel I must recount an interview, which I had with an old lady of 90 in 1960, for a radio programme. Her name was Mrs. Hammond, of 10 North Great George's Street. Her story concerned the Invincibles and the deaths of Cavendish and Burke in the Park in 1882, when she was twelve. 'The next day was Sunday, and me and another girl went up along the main road of the Park, until we found the spot, where the men had been killed. The two of us gathered seven stones, that had blood on them, in our pinnies (bibs), and when we got home, my mother murdered me, and her mother murdered her for doing such a thing. Then my mother got a spade and dug a hole in a field at the back of the Mater Hospital — it was open country then — and buried the stones and the pinnies.'

The greatest event to take place in the Phoenix Park during my boyhood was the Centenary of Catholic Emancipation in 1929. It seemed to me as if the whole world's population had come to the 'Fifteen Acres' for this commemoration. And when one remembered the dark days of the Penal Laws it was fitting and right to celebrate.

The Hollow in the Phoenix Park.

12 Early Dublin Picturehouses

The 'Mayro' — The 'Lousebank' — The 'Manor', the 'Tivo' and the 'Fizzer' — The 'Fountain' and the 'Eleck' — The 'Feeno' — A visit to the 'Mayro' — The Penny Rush — Woodeners and Cushioners — 'Show the Pictures!' — Tom Mix — 'We don't care.'

THERE WAS A rash of picturehouses in Dublin after the First World War. They popped up all over the place and all became known by shortened versions of their real names. The best known was the 'Mayro' that is, the Mary Street Picturehouse, the entrance to which was at the junction of Mary Street and Wolfe Tone Street.

In Mary Street, also, was the Lyceum, originally the Volta, but known to all the kids of Dublin as the 'Lousebank'. This was the picturehouse managed by James Joyce in the early part of the century. Many of us managed to get in here quite often for free. The eight-penny tram ticket to Dalkey was identical in size, shape and colour with the tickets used in the 'Lousebank'. This dodge worked for a while, until they changed the tickets. 'Hey, Muttoner, keep a seat for me inside.'

Then there was the 'Manor' or 'Broadway' in Manor Street, the 'Tivo' in Francis Street, the 'Roto' i.e. the Rotunda down town, the 'Fizzer' at Blacquire Bridge, the 'Fountain' in James's Street, the 'Eleck' in Talbot Street. Last, but not least, was the 'Feeno' i.e. the Phoenix Picture Palace on Ellis Quay. As I said, the 'Mayro' was the best known; the admission fee in the Twenties was threepence, pronounced 'trupence'.

The 'Mayro' was so popular that both grown-ups and youngsters came from the south side of the city to it. The only cheap picturehouse that I myself attended on the south

119

Corner of Mary and Wolfe Tone Street, the former 'Mayro' Cinema.

The Broadway, Manor Street.

120

side was the Camden in Camden Street. This was the picture-house where everybody walked in backwards, owing to the position of the screen.

All of these picturehouses were cheap ones. There were in town, of course, the 'swanky' ones with cushioned seats everywhere. These were the La Scala in Prince's Street, the Grand Central in O'Connell Street, the Grafton in Grafton Street, the Metropole and the Sackville in O'Connell Street and the Corinthian on the Quay.

However, the Penny Rush was the big event of the week. Some people say that the Penny Rush was originally a South City feature in the Abercorn. I do not dispute that, but I can tell them that THE Penny Rush took place every Saturday in the late Teens and early Twenties at the Phoenix Cinema on Ellis Quay. This was the building affectionately known as 'The Feeno'. Dublin kids, the majority of them boys, came from the four corners of the Metropolis to the 'Feeno' for this cheap showing of pictures. The queue usually rounded the complete block, covering Queen Street, Benburb Street and John Street plus Ellis Quay itself. The cinema was built to hold about 450, but for the Penny Rush I would say about 3,000 children presented themselves every Saturday. And everybody got in; I always did. The crowds were so big and unruly that the attendants – as we called them – Mr. McCabe and Mr. Bennett used to keep the lines in order with a cane. It was swished without mercy and everybody toed the line. Two hawkers, one of them named Bridie, sold oranges and apples to this army of boys. The peels were used as ammunition inside. As we filed in we put our pennies on a table, watched by door-man Morrissy. Inside the cinema itself was chaos plus pandemonium. The noise was ear-splitting. Everybody seemed to be shouting the name of some pal lost in the queueing up outside. To the shouts of 'Where are yez?' came the inevitable, 'We're over here.'

At the Penny Rush, there was no class distinction. For a penny you were put into either the 'Woodeners', the 'Cushioners' or the 'Upstairs', according to your place in the queue. Tony and myself and the others of our group always made sure never to get seated in the rows down-stairs, which were immediately under the front line of the balcony. As nobody could go to the toilet during the show –

121

even the aisles were jammed — for fear of losing his place, most boys relieved themselves where they were. The boys in the front row of the balcony performed this feat down on the boys beneath. Downstairs, the floor was built at a slant and the accumulated urine trickled its way down to where the old lady played the piano. She always played that famous William Tell piece for the chase at the end. Looking back I do not know how the poor woman stood the stench.

As all the young patrons came in groups from different parts of the city, the time before the start of the film was passed with miniature wars and fights in and out among the seats. Sometimes a struggling pair was dragged out by an attendant to the shouts of 'Hit him up; he's no relation!'

Then suddenly, and without warning, the cinema was plunged into darkness and the pictures started. At this point a cheer went up that put the combined Dalymount, Croke Park and Lansdowne Road roars in the shade. When a picture broke down a similar roar commenced: 'Show the pictures!' The most popular pictures of those grand years were 'The Hooded Terror' and 'Elmo, King of the Jungle', Pearl White we loved in the serials, or 'Follyinuppers'. William S. Hart was king of the cowboys until Tom Mix came along. Fatty Arbuckle and Charlie Chaplin always put us in stitches, as did Lloyd Hamilton and his cap and Buster Keaton. Larry Semon and Harold Lloyd were great favourites of my own. One serious picture, I remember clearly was 'The Ten Commandments' with Richard Dix.

In every picture at the Penny Rush there was a chase at the end, and the loud cheering always drowned the noise of the piano. Those were the days when kids really lived the stories. They never sat quietly through a screen fight. Each boy dug into his neighbour and synchronised his blows with that of the 'chap's'. In every film there was always a 'chap', a 'girl' and 'villyun'.

A black man's appearance on the screen always brought shouts of 'Soap! soap!'. The sight of the 'villyun' creeping up behind the 'chap' or 'girl' brought frenzied cries of 'Look behind!' One thing that makes me smile when I look back on silent films, and that is the reading of the captions and dialogue. *Everybody* read aloud the printed words, and I mean *everybody*.

The pictures were very real to us, because they were a new thing in our lives and Hooded Terrors were to be found in every school-yard. We certainly never noticed any technical faults. Recently I was reminded by a friend of a picture in which Tom Mix had been put in jail by the sheriff. Outside was Tom's horse, Tony. Tom whistled and Tony moved up to the window. Tom took the rope from the saddle, tied one end to the bars of the window and the other end to the horse. He then gave Tony a slap on the hindquarters. Tony galloped off and pulled down the whole jail. How we wished to have a horse like Tony.

On the way to the 'Feeno' it was the custom to call into Lane's shop in Queen Street to have a go on the penny slot-machines. In there, one always found the 'know-all' who maintained that he knew the art of manipulating the machine successfully. He was the cause of many lost pennies and more rows, and Mr. Lane himself or Josie had to take a hand.

Sweets for the pictures were bought in Dinny Gogan's, two doors from Lanes. This was a shop, where sweets were manufactured in the basement, and the smell coming up through the grating was heavenly. In Dinny's a boy could buy a ha'porth of crumbs, a sugary conglomeration of small bits and pieces of all kinds of sweets. On Saturdays he seemed to have plenty of crumbs.

Regarding the wars and fights inside of the 'Feeno', I can remember one particular tussle in the 'Upstairs', between a big brawny fellow and a small weasel of a boy, who was barefooted. To shouts of 'Hit your match', the big fellow lifted the small lad, and shoved him over the balcony ledge. Fortunately, the centre aisle was jammed with boys and he fell unhurt on top of these. Up he jumped again, fought his way out through the door, up the stairs and was at it hammer and tongs with the big fellow once more, until both were dragged apart and thrown out on the quays.

Girls were always a minority group, but those who came were just as tough as the boys. They fought their way to good vantage points. They pulled the hair of boys, who got in their way, while their screams during the more exciting parts of the picture mingled with the shouts of the boys to produce a dreadful cacophony.

The Penny Rush was certainly not a nursery of gentleness,

The 'Feeno' on Ellis Quay.

yet I am sure many of our more respected and solid citizens of today will smile at what I write and say, 'Ah yes, I was there, too'. There is a well-known Dominican priest, who will laugh to read of the Hooded Terror and there is also a Christian Brother who will derive extra special pleasure from the story of the boy being pushed over the balcony. He was the small barefooted boy.

Coming home from the Penny Rush was also a movement full of life and exuberance. As we lived close by, we were just spectators at this stage. Groups and little gangs from the different districts of Dublin reformed, and after a few mild skirmishes went their different ways singing football songs like:

'We don't care whether we win, lose or draw,
For all the hell we care
For all we know there's goin' to be a match,
And it's good old (Team name) will be there.'

These finished with shouts of 'Lurry them up' and 'Wheel them in'. And as the boys marched home singing their nonsense songs, the older people at their doors threw up their hands and asked, 'What are the children nowadays coming to?'

The Phoenix Cinema is no more. Never again will they come from as far away as Fairview, Ringsend or Drumcondra in little groups and converge on Ellis Quay, as if drawn by a magnet. Television, radio, bingo and the new pubs wiped out the Penny Rush; but I can never pass along Ellis Quay without seeing, with memory's eye, the burly form of Mr. McCabe, moving along an endless line of boyhood, waving his cane and shouting, 'So yez won't line up, won't yez'.

All the other old picturehouses have disappeared. The buildings are still there, but factories, garages and offices have taken over. I wonder if the workers in these places ever hear ghostly shouts of 'Show the Pictures!'.

Some of the games we played are still being played by boys, games like 'Relieveo', which needs no description. One game, which has disappeared is 'Cap on the Back', a sophisticated version of 'leap-frog. As each member of one team leap-frogged over a boy's back, he left his cap until there was a pile of caps. The last over had to lift the pile, while leap-frogging without knocking any cap to the ground.

We played 'Follow the Leader' also. This game always got us into trouble, as the leader was always tempted to do daring things, like knocking at doors, or pulling down placards, or shouting nicknames into shops. And it was those at the end of the line who were caught and blamed.

Marbles were very popular. We played games which are now forgotten e.g. 'French', 'Dab', 'Folly' and 'Hole and Taw'. A large marble was a taw and some boys were fortunate enough to have steel marbles, which were huge ball-bearings in reality. To play 'French' two players were enough. Each placed a marble at the edge of the path, and striking his taw against the wall tried to direct it towards one of the marbles. If he struck one, and knocked it off the path, he claimed it for himself and his opponent had to put one of his marbles in the empty place. Such a game as this went on for a long time. 'Have yous chiselers nuttin' to do but play marbles?' 'Dab' was different. The players put their marbles – one each – in a cluster near the wall. Next the owners took turns at taking two or three steps towards the cluster from about ten feet away and aiming and throwing (as in darts) their taws at the marbles. Each marble struck became the property of the striker.

The most enjoyable game was 'Hole and Taw'. Players took turns to roll their taws into a hole in the road. There were two holes, usually about six feet apart. Each player tried to keep the others from rolling their taws into the holes. After reaching the first hole, a player aimed towards the second, after which he returned to the first hole. Having entered the first hole, he was entitled to strike any of the other taws in order to drive them off course. First back to base was the winner.

The only marble game that still remains at the present day is 'Folly', in which one marble is rolled after another until it strikes. If a boy struck a marble with his own, he was given a marble in payment. This game was played usually on the way home from school. To prevent a rival striking his marble an incantation was used. Moving the hand in circles over his waiting marble the owner chanted, 'Bit o' moss round that marble, Bit o' moss round that marble'.

Boys' pockets were loaded with marbles, and very often a large taw or steel marble or a leadener was exchanged for ten or twelve marbles, or more. Mrs. Cullen sold marbles in her shop for five a penny. The season for playing marbles was February — just before Lent.

Besides marbles there were tops. Mrs. Cullen sold both tops and whips. The whips sold in the shops were not very strong, and not very good, so many of us made our own. Whips were a common sight in the area due to the large horse population. The tops season was an extraordinary one. We lashed our tops in groups and some of the boys became very skilful with them, on a par, I would say, with the skills of latter-day children with yo-yos. The roadway was not suitable for a spinning top on account of the cobblestones. Our favourite place was the waste ground in Smithfield, where a boy could lash his top a great distance on the fairly level, tarred roadway. The top was spun first with the hand, although some boys twined the whip-cord around it to start it. Some boys could raise the top in the air and bring it down still spinning about twenty feet away. The whole purpose of top-spinning was to keep it spinning and this brought in a competitive element. I remember keeping a top spinning for almost an hour. I can remember Brendan McKeown, lifting a top with one lash, and sending it from the path outside Scanlan's the saddler over to the path outside Mr. McAuley's house at No. 7.

We also had hoops. The usual hoop was the rim of a bicycle wheel and this was propelled along with a stick or a wire. We used to run in gangs around the blocks of houses in 'Follow the Leader' style. One day our gang 'hooped' it up to the Gough Monument and back. 'Give us a bowl of your hoop, Hobby.'

As already mentioned there was a stretch of level tarry ground at the south east corner of Smithfield, where we played most of our ball games. We called it 'the waste ground' and horse-owners of the area used it for training young horses. I derived great pleasure from watching these young horses going round and round in a circle with young Joe Fagan in the centre, holding the reins and cracking the whip. It was like the circus to us.

We played Rounders on this waste ground; this was a very popular game in Dublin in the mid-Twenties. Caps or coats were used to mark the four quarters. We also played a kind of cricket. The wicket was marked on Jameson's wall with tar by Frannie Roche (the wicket was still there in 1979). When we played football the game was soccer mainly, because there was less chance of losing or 'canting' the ball. A ball, a rubber one, cost fourpence, but very often we made do with a rag one, tied lightly with strong string.

However, there were other pastimes besides street games; I am referring to reading and outdoor sports like swimming.

Once I had learned to read I could never get enough books. However, before I joined Thomas Street and Capel Street Libraries I had to go through the comics stage. The comic-cuts were bought in Lane's shop in Queen Street from Josie, or in Maguire's in Benburb Street from Mrs. Maguire herself. She was very popular with children because she was kind. And she was a great friend of my mother.

I read *Funny Wonder* which was coloured blue, *Chips,* which had a pink colour, *Merry and Bright,* which was yellow, *Tiger Tim's Weekly,* which was multi-coloured, *Film Fun,* which was white, and *The Rainbow,* which was multi-coloured. They cost one penny each. Later came the *Wizard,* the forerunner of the *Beano,* and the *Magnet.* I did enjoy Billy Bunter and the Greyfriars gang, but there was one magazine which I never failed to get. This was *Our Boys,* which had been launched in the year after my own birth. It cost 3d., was published fortnightly and was crammed with stories all of which had an Irish Ireland slant. We got them from the Brother in the school; the money was collected on Fridays. 'Stand out to the line the boys, who didn't pay for *Our Boys.*'

Later, I went through all the Edgar Wallace books of mystery and crime. Regarding the comic-cuts, I earned a reputation for having all of the comics, so there was a constant knocking at our door by 'swoppers'. Besides my own playmates, I often found strangers on the doorstep asking to swap a *Funny Wonder* for a *Merry and Bright*.

My mother never tired of telling of one particular boy from Blackhall Street. He was small and barefooted. When he knocked at our door with the two comic-cuts under his arm, my mother opened the door to him. Surprised, as he was expecting me, he took a pace back; then standing in a boastful, cocksure way stated:

'We had an egg!'

'You had an egg?' (My mother said this incredulously, as eggs were 7d. each at the time.)

'Me father had one and we all got a bit.'

I had three tickets in each of the two libraries, Thomas Street and Capel Street. I continued on with fiction stories like *Treasure Island* and *Kidnapped,* but I reached the stage later when I was willing to read any kind of book. These ranged from travel to autobiographies. Most of my reading was done in the kitchen as reading by candle-light was rather frustrating. However the outdoor pastimes were the more appealing.

After the Truce in 1922 a group of about five of us used to go swimming in the Tolka. To reach our destination, we had to walk up Stoneybatter and Prussia Street to Old Cabra Road. From this point on we were in open country. Turning at the crossroads, outside the entrance to St. Joseph's School for the Deaf, and offering a prayer for Tom Breslin's uncle, Christy, who was killed by the Tans here, we hurried down Ratoath Road, which was really a hedged country lane. 'When you see a cow on its own in a field — that's a bull.' We passed the entrance to the Blind Lane and the water pump and cottages on our left — on the right was a large white-washed farmhouse and here we turned right with the road. We hurried here because on the other side of the road which led to the Dominican Convent, was Lord Norbury's house. The house was supposed to be haunted, and we were willing to believe anything after hearing that he was called the Hanging Judge. A stone head of a man was fixed on the front wall of that house. Having rounded the corner, we next turned left and up the hill towards Broombridge. There was a brand new bungalow on our left here, and blackberry bushes all the way up to and over the bridge of the Royal Canal. From here on we ran down the steep hill to the road at the bottom. Crossing this, we entered a short cul-de-sac and climbed a gate into a field, through which the Tolka flowed. There was a pool here called the Scout's Hat. Further up the river were other pools called the Silverspoon and the Broken Arch. The cul-de-sac itself led to a very deep quarry, from which we kept far away. We believed it had no bottom. 'Last in is a Molly.'

The days were always sunny then, or was it my imagination? We lazed away the days here getting in for about half a dozen swims. All of the group, Tony, the two Stynes, Kevin Costello, Michael Lyons and myself could swim in a kind of way. I suppose one could say that we thought we could swim. This was the early Twenties.

Later on, we graduated to Broombridge itself, where the great test was to cross the canal in one dive. Years later, around 1928 and 1929 I joined with Martin Daly, Frank Harrington (Harro), Frank Barron and Jackie Hunter to go swimming near Ashtown. I can remember watching with envy the smooth Australian Crawl of Dessie Fricker.

By 1927 we all had bicycles of some sort and our journey was made along Blackhorse Lane, where we called at Tuite's thatched cottage to buy apples. As we waited for our apples, we admired the lovely dresser full of shining delf in the kitchen. The lovely old-fashioned cottage is an idiosyncrasy today, surrounded by three-storey luxury flats. It is Oisín i ndiaidh na Féinne in earnest.

Another swimming haunt of ours was the Liffey, behind the church in Chapelizod. We reached this point by cycling along the tow-path from Islandbridge. Another reason for liking this place was the presence of an orchard owned by Flanagans on the north bank beside the church. After crossing the Liffey, and taking some apples, we returned to the tow-path on the south side.

The seaside attracted us also and with different groups I often paid 2d. return to go to Blackrock by train. Seapoint I also visited, but the best place of all was Dollymount — Dollier.

'Can you dive?'
'Of course I can!'
'Let's see you — '

'That's not a dive, that's a bellier.'

'Can you swim?'
'Yeh, like a brick.'
We swam of course in Tara Street Baths but I never liked them.

In the summertime we often went on outings, to the Phoenix Park maybe or to Merrion. Our mothers never objected, and we took our grub with us. I remember going one day to a place called the Private Woods near Ashtown. The Tolka flowed past our picnic spot and we had a great day. The farthest journey we ever made was to the Pine Forest. We travelled by tram from the Pillar to Rathfarnham and trekked the rest of the way on foot. It was a beautiful day and we had a wonderful time. This was one of the many episodes that made up a happy childhood.
'At last we reached the mountains,
We were starvin', fit to fall,
Hobby filled the kettle,
An' we all got sticks an' all.
"We'll make a smashin' fire" said Cock,
"Then we'll have a game of 'Catch'."
But when we went to light it —
Janey, no one had a match.'

14. Altar-boys of St. Paul's

Joining the altar-boys — Priests in St. Paul's — Learning to serve — Benediction and the Thurifer — The altar-boys — Up in the belfry — On the altar — Latin pronunciation — Forty Hours — Retreats — The Seven Churches — Annual treat — Altar Boys' League — Upstairs, Downstairs and Upstarts.

I JOINED THE altar-boys of St. Paul's, Arran Quay in 1921, when I was almost eight. My brother, Martin, had been 'on the altar' for about two years before me. My mother made our surplices and soutanes; these were a bright purple. The Mass, of course, was the Latin Mass and Terry Lyons of the Haymarket, who was a senior altar-boy, took on the job of teaching the Latin responses to myself and about four others. Sometimes he brought us into his home to do this.

When Canon Fagan the Parish Priest died, he was succeeded by Fr. Eugene McCarthy. He was the priest who married Joseph Mary Plunkett and Grace Gifford in Kilmainham Jail before Plunkett's execution. He was a red-faced man, with a rather proud bearing. However, he was a nice priest and so was Father Martin. Fr. Martin was the priest who had married my father and mother. Éamon de Valera and Sinéad Ní Fhlannagáin had been married in the same church a couple of days before them. Phibsboro', where the Flanagans lived, was in St. Paul's Parish.

Another priest was Fr. Condren, who had thick, white, curly hair into which he rubbed vaseline. His biretta always had a layer of the stuff around the edge. We all liked him, but not one of the altar-boys liked Fr. McDonald. A black-haired priest with a very white face, he treated the boys as if they were slaves. The two boys scheduled to serve his Mass had to stand behind him as he robed and help him to fix his vest-

134

ST. PAUL'S R.C. CHAPEL. DUBLIN .1199. W.L.

St. Paul's Church, Arran Quay, as it used to be.

ments properly. A wrong move earned a clatter on the ear. We were very glad when he was transferred.

The other priests, Fr. Mulcahy, Fr. Fitzgibbon and Fr. Herlihy, were attached to the parish, but they lived on Cabra Road, opposite St. Peter's Church. Their duties lay in the Cabra, Phibsboro' and Glasnevin areas because St. Paul's Parish at this time was the largest parish in the city. Fr. Fitzgibbon was the most popular of these.

I was shivering with fear the first time I went out on the High Altar with Willie Fitzpatrick. Willie, being a senior, took the right hand side where the bell was. The boy on the bell-side led the way in all movements, like changing the missal from one side to the other for the Gospel. I joined him, of course, for the pouring of the wine and water. Kneeling on the altar-step that first morning, I felt that everybody was watching me. I joined Willie in the responses and when we were preceding Fr. Martin back to the Sacristy I heaved a sigh of relief.

The next four Masses I served with Mossy my brother who, of course, was an experienced Mass-server at this time. Then came the day when I was allowed to take my position on the bell-side. I know I rang the bell too soon once, but nobody mentioned anything about it. After that the sky was the limit. In fact, I had now reached the stage when I could serve Mass on my own.

The number of altar-boys was very large. On Sundays at the last Mass six servers often lined up and, of course, a big team was needed for Benediction. There were many squabbles about who should be acolyte or who should be on the Monstrance. This was all settled when the most senior boy, Bernie Fitzpatrick, was put in charge of us. He drew up a list for every day. Later on Danny Maher from the Confraternity took over and did the same thing. 'Anyone who disobeys will be put off the altar.'

For Benediction, the boy on the Thurible had the job of getting the charcoal reddened. This was done at the fire or with matches or candles. Besides the Acolytes and the Thurifer, there was the Incense boy, the boy for the Alb and, of course, the Monstrance boy. The three hymns were always in Latin: 'O Salutaris', 'Tantum Ergo' and 'Adoremus'.

Before Bernie Fitzpatrick was made head altar-boy there

were many squabbles about who should do what:

'I'm on thurible tonight.'

'Oh no, you're not; I haven't had my turn.'

'It's Noel's chance.'

'It isn't; he's only an acolyte' (newcomer)

'Looka, ask anyone; it's my turn.'

'Do the monstrance and you can be thurifer next week.'

'I'm not doing the monstrance; but I'll do the cope.'

'Oh no you won't; Joey is down for that.'

'Who pur 'im down; I'm goin' to see the Clerk.'

'Oh alright, you do thurible; but who's goin' to do the incense?'

'Johnny will, he likes doin' that.'

'Where's the charcoal?'

'Find it yourself. You said you wanted to do thurible.'

'Here light that candle; the fire is no use.'

On Sundays and on Church Holy days, there was always a strong smell of burning incense in and around the Sacristy. We often put incense on the charcoal, merely to watch the smoke and experience the smell, which I always found pleasant.

Some of the other altar-boys were Noel Fitzpatrick, a brother of Bernie and Willie, Dick Conroy, Joey Ward, Gerry Dunn, Tommy O'Gorman, John Keatley, John Kavanagh, Jimmy Kane, Michael Bannon, Tom McInerney, 'Totch' McGrath, Michael Hogan, a boy named Donohue from the sweet-shop in North Brunswick Street, John Hanway, Terry Lyons, Jimmy Somers, Charlie Somers, Tom Flynn, John Keatley, Paddy and Roddy Reid, John Cummins and Jimmy Whelan.

As mentioned before, we had to supply our own soutanes, but there were always old ones in the big press in the Sacristy, left behind by altar-boys who had retired. They were happy days, and like all happy days, they passed all too quickly. We had great fun sitting and talking about the 'Feeno' and the 'Mayro' around the gas-fire. Stealing the bread hosts was our main offence. They always tasted so nice, better than ordinary bread — due to the thinness, I suppose. I remember being sent with Dick Conroy out to Roebuck, Blackrock, to an enclosed order of nuns to collect two parcels of new breads. We went on our bikes. The parcels were handed out to us through a small grid, and all we saw was a hand. 'If she sees yeh, she'll get trun out o' the convent.'

There were lots of other chores done by altar-boys. Mossy and I often helped Jimmy Byrne, the clerk, to take in the flower vases, or to light the tall candles with a taper, or fill the cruets with water for the next Mass. One thing we all loved to do was ring the bell for Devotions in the months of May and October. We took our turns in groups of three and four. As soon as the bell got into a rhythm of peals we took turns to grab the rope. Up we were taken through the hole in the belfry-room ceiling and down again. It was a wonderful feeling. The Bong! Bong! of the bell was deafening.

On our way down from the belfry we met old Tom Clarke on his way up to pump the organ for Miss Maxwell and the choir. The lever for the organ-pump was hidden behind a projection at the side of the organ-loft. The old organ had to be pumped before and after the Rosary, and during the Benediction, of course.

High Mass was a very important event and much time was spent on rehearsal. Every boy got a job to do; the newcomers were made acolytes, as it was the easiest task. The choir, also, had to do a great deal of rehearsing. This was done either in the Sacristy or in the rooms upstairs. The two most prominent singers in the Arran Quay choir were Teresa Owens and Mr. Fricker, the bass.

> 'I'n an altar-boy for six months now,
> I can serve Mass on me own,
> When I joined I knew no Latin,
> T'wasn't long till I was shown.
> An' now I know me way about,
> I do things very well,
> An' every day when Mass is said,
> I'n the one that rings the bell.'

Altar-boys in Arran Quay were noted for some irreverent pronunciations of the Latin e.g. 'A dame quickly killed a cat, shoot him shoot him ma'am'. (Ad Deum, qui laetificat juventutem meam). 'O rap your nose, Miss' (Ora pro nobis). 'I'm a cowboy, I'm a cowboy, I'm a Mexican cowboy.' (Mea culpa, mea culpa, mea maxima culpa). 'She cut a rat in the G.P.O.' (Sicut erat in principio).

Altar-boys of St. Pauls 1924 — Martin and Paddy Crosbie extreme left front row.

The Forty Hours Adoration was very important also. We worked according to a list and we had to go in twos. Each pair had to spend one hour before the altar. The altar was always a picture of brilliance. It was made of wood in collapsible tiers on which were placed lines of vases with flowers and dozens of candles. The Monstrance holding the Blessed Sacrament was enveloped in a veritable blaze of light and colour. As I knelt on the kneeler, I heard the constant shuffling of people in the church behind me. This became very pronounced after tea, that is, when the work of the day was over.

Altar-boys were present at all of the Retreats and, of course, we heard all of the sermons intended for the grown-ups both men and women. The missioners certainly had an effect on all present, because the queues for Confession lasted the whole week. One thing I noticed about the two missioners — one was always much better than the other. That is, there was always one good preacher and one mediocre one. The sermons on mortal sin and hell frightened us altar-boys. However, there were nice quiet sermons also, and I can still remember the sermon on Our Lady, given by Fr. Austin.

'What did the Missioner say about Mortal Sin?'

'He was against it.'

Holy Thursday was a big night for Dubliners during the Twenties. Both young and old continued a custom that must have been carried on for generations. I refer to the custom of visiting seven churches. Nobody seemed to know the reason for this custom, but the streets during the late evening were chock-a-block with groups of people hurrying from one church to another. As an altar-boy I was confined to Arran Quay on a couple of Holy Thursdays, but I did manage to do the seven on many occasions, particularly after leaving the altar. 'How many churches have yez done?' The altars were adorned and decorated in the same way as for the Forty Hours Adoration. The theme of all conversation was the altars, and there were hot arguments as to which was the best. I remember visiting Stanhope Street Convent Chapel, Church Street, George's Hill Convent Chapel, St. Michan's, Arran Quay, John's Lane and Meath Street. The two convent chapel altars were always the best. 'The nuns have nothing else to do', someone said. I have questioned boys in recent years about the old custom, and not one single boy had even heard of it.

Twice a year we were given a treat, an outing to the seaside in the summer and a visit to the pantomime in the Gaiety or Olympia in the winter. On one of our outings, we went to Portmarnock and it became an important day for me. John Keatley's father came with the group, and he spent quite a while teaching me how to swim. Before that sunny day, I believed I was able to swim, but crossing the canal or the broken arch in one dive wasn't really swimming. Now (1924) I could really swim.

The outings and treats were memorable in many ways. We bought cigarettes and smoked them on the way back from the panto. One year instead of a panto treat, we were brought to the Grand Central Cinema in O'Connell Street. Once again we showed how grown-up we were by smoking cigarettes. After the shows we came back to the rooms over the Sacristy, where Jimmy Byrne lived with his family. There we were given a slap-up tea by Mrs. Byrne.

In the Twenties there was an Altar-boys' League in which we took part. It was a soccer league and our team wasn't much good. The matches were played in the Fifteen Acres, and altar-boys from all over the city took part. Jimmy Byrne, the clerk of the chapel, managed the team, which lasted about two years. One day, we were scheduled to play Clarendon Street in the Phoenix Park. Both teams arrived on time. On the ground next to ours two teams — not altar-boys — were all ready and waiting to start. However, no referee had arrived. Both captains approached a passer-by, and after some time persuaded him to take on the job. The game commenced and so did ours. After about ten minutes, there was a terrific rumpus on the other pitch. Evidently, the decisions of the new referee did not seem fair to either side, and the next thing we saw was the poor man running like mad across the Fifteen Acres and both teams after him.

There was a positive class distinction in most of the Catholic churches during my boyhood. In Arran Quay itself, there was a barrier rail separating the Body of the church from the Sanctuary. The offering at the Sanctuary door was 2d.; the offering at the doors to the Body and the Gallery was 1d. Holy Communion was administered first to those in the Sanctuary; then the priest proceeded down to the dividing rails to the so-called lower class. In the Sanctuary were publicans, shopkeepers, businessmen and their families, plus those who thought they were a cut above their neighbours. This division was something that I noticed and resented, even as a boy, and after joining the altar society, I noticed something else. Even among the altar-boys there was an indefinable division between sons of shopkeepers and publicans and sons of ordinary working people. The former kept together in a group; they went to the large picture-houses down town and had never been at the Penny Rush in the Feeno.

Many of the priests were seen to hob-nob with the moneyed section of the community, and were frequent visitors to their houses. All of the priests were not of this breed; Fr. Byrne and Fr. Martin were often in our house. Fr. Mulcahy called on two occasions – for the Dues.

No boy ever refused to serve a Nuptial Mass, because on such occasions we were given money by the best man. These 'tips' were usually in the region of two shillings or half-a-crown. One day I served such a Mass for two tinkers; I got no 'tip'. Fr. McCarthy used go into a rage over the confetti in the chapel yard, and no matter how often he complained from the pulpit, people carried on as if he'd said nothing.

On the days before Palm Sunday it was the custom for altar-boys to help in the breaking up of the palm into small pieces. We used knives and small hatchets for this chore. When Sunday morning came the palm was arranged in large baskets, and given to the people going to and coming from the Masses. Arran Quay Church was packed for every Mass, because of the huge population in the area. At the late Masses on Sunday the congregation spilled out onto the steps of the church itself, and the stairs leading to the gallery always had a full quota. It is sad to see the old church nowadays locked and bolted all day, and opened only at Mass-time at 10 a.m.

Life was certainly full for me. Movement was non-stop and the word 'bored' was never heard of. However, no matter what we were doing, Mossy, Mona, and myself were always in time for meals. We always toed the line for my mother, and a respect for punctuality has stayed with me all through my life.

15 Messages, Shops and Little Jobs

Loose milk — Mrs. Cullen's shop — Friday night was pay night — Peggy's Leg and Vimto — Buttermilk — Coal — Rice's — Reilly's shop — Mrs. Maguire — Heather's on the quay — 'Four ounces of butter, please!' — Butter-boxes — Minding horses — 'Hey Mister, Your horse is gone' — 'A little bit off the back and sides'.

THERE WAS NO such thing as bottled milk in the Twenties. A common sight to see was boys and girls wending their way at tea-time to the dairy shops, all armed with large jugs. Big gulps were taken from the jugs on the way home. Mossy or Mona or myself were sent for pints or quarts to Murphy's of Phoenix Street or the Dainty Dairy or Cork Dairy, both of which were in Queen Street. In the later Twenties, we had a regular milkman, who delivered the milk to our door. His name was Jonathan and like all milkmen, he gave an extra sup called a Tilly, from the Irish word tuille, which means more or extra. 'I'm sure that oul' fella waters the milk.'

The loose milk, as it was called, went sour very quickly in the warm weather. There were no fridges, and sour milk was always a problem. We were also sent to the shops for fresh bread and always arrived home with a large hole eaten from one side. 'I'll take your sacred life, if you do that again.'

My mother had a weekly account with Mrs. Cullen of No. 5 Haymarket, that is, we 'dealt' with Mrs. Cullen. At Christmas, she always gave us a large candle and a Christmas cake — it was a Dublin custom for shopkeepers to present regulars with a Christmas box. Our weekly bill was always paid on Friday, when my father got his wages. Each of us loved to be sent to pay this bill; the reward was a chocolate bar or toffee.

Going for the milk.

'When me father brins his wages home,
At tea-time, Friday night,
I run out and get the milk
An' the table-cloth's snow white.
Me mother gives him two boiled eggs,
An' the fire is grand and bright,
When me father brins his wages home,
At tea-time, Friday night.

Me mother cuts the envelope
An' she burns it on the hob,
She counts out all the money,
An' me father gets ten bob.
We all gather 'round him,
We say nuttin', nor a ting,
An' he says nuttin' neither,
But he gives us each a 'wing'.

"Don't forget the Diddley,
Last week we didn't pay,"
Me father tells me mother this,
He tells her every day.
She puts the money in a vase,
That she keeps up on the shelf;
I think she keeps it all in there,
'Cause I've looked in there meself.'

From Mrs. Cullen we bought bread, tea, sugar, biscuits and cakes. All of the Haymarket boys bought their sweets from her. Peggy's Leg was one ha'penny, Sharps Kreemy Toffee cost one penny, Aniseed Balls were sixteen a penny, bullseyes twelve a penny, fizz bags cost one ha'penny, and the popular drink Vimto was twopence. A penny bought five marbles, or two liquorice pipes. A peashooter cost a ha'penny.

Whenever we needed eggs, I was sent around to the Cork Dairy in Queen Street, over which the Stynes family lived. Mr. Murphy owned the dairy, and his eggs were 8d. a dozen. I often called into the Cork Dairy myself for a half gallon of buttermilk, which cost three ha'pence. Whenever I could, I bought buttermilk for myself all during the Twenties, in fact, right up to the time we left the district. I had developed a craze for this drink, after my father had given me a taste of it one day in a friend's house.

We bought our coal by the stone sometimes in Rice's of Benburb Street. It was as much as I could carry at one time, so I had to make about half a dozen journeys to lay in a store. Old Mrs. Rice herself weighed out the coal, and it cost 3d. per stone. For vegetables, either Mona or myself was sent to Reilly's shop on the corner of Hendrick Lane in Benburb Street. Hogan's pub was on the other corner. We were always warned to go to Big Mary, who always gave everything with a heavy hand. This was a very popular shop and I always had to queue up, although there were four daughters serving in the shop, along with Mrs. Reilly herself.

I bought my comic-cuts and magazines in Maguires of Benburb Street or Lanes of Queen Street. Lanes was a bigger shop and had slot machines and Josie, who served there, was a very nice person. However, I always tried Maguire's first, because Mrs. Maguire was a friend of my mother, and always had a query for me about school. Another thing, in the matter of sweets, she always seemed to put in an extra one. 'A ha'porth of aniseed balls and a Peggy's Leg, please.'

Our chemists were either Checkett's of Queen Street or Fitzpatrick's of Stoneybatter. My mother favoured the latter, but it was a much longer journey than to Checketts, which was almost opposite Dolan's pub. Mr. Checkett lived in Clondalkin. 'Checkett the feckit, the Rick Stick Steckit.'

There was a very popular drapery shop on Arran Quay in the Twenties. The name was Heather's and it was quite a large shop. My mother went there quite often and I liked to go with her and watch the aerial boxes which were used to convey money from the counter to the cashier's office. The change came back in this same box along the wire without much delay. Inside also was the receipt. It was always a mystery to me how these small circular boxes could speed along the wires. There were always chairs at the counters for the customers.

One day my mother went down to Heather's on her own and on her return at tea-time told the family a funny story about a beggar, who had parked himself outside of St. Paul's Church. He had his cap held out in front of him, and as my mother approached he said in a loud voice, 'May the blessings of God follow you.' As my mother reached him he added

Heathers of Arran Quay (1928).

'Wherever you go.' When my mother had passed him and was evidently not going to give him anything, he shouted after her his final phrase, 'And may they never catch up with you.'

Whenever my mother wanted ice-cream she sent us to Killeens in Queen Street — this was next door to the Blanchardstown Mills. We got meat in Eastman's or in Neilan's at No. 76 in Queen Street. There was a pork butchers next-door to Neilan's named Hick's. 'Run over to Hick's and get me a pound of sausages and make sure he gives you long ones.'

There was a hardware shop at the corner of Hendrick Street. I don't ever remember being inside this shop. Most of the items were of a farming nature and the owner was a Mr. Purcell, who wore a hat in the shop. Hendrick Street was a place I did not like, not on account of the Hentown gang, who were our 'enemies', but on account of the terrible smell, which wafted its way in every direction from Judd's, the skin and hide factory. My father often made the crack about the man who was hiding from the police because he skinned everybody. It took me a long time to understand the connection between Judd's, the word 'hiding' and the word 'skinned'.

After the Civil War my mother commenced to do her week-end shopping in Thomas Street, which was only a short distance from our house. The shop she visited regularly was the Mayo Provision Stores near the corner of Meath Street. On occasions I was sent on messages to the same shop. There was a thin-faced youth in the place at this time; I think he had started as a messenger boy. Little did I realise that he and I would be working together in the Capitol Theatre twenty years later. He was the much-loved comedian Mike Nolan (R.I.P.)

Laundry was done for us by another Thomas Street shop, the Harold's Cross Laundry, whose shop was just around the corner from the top of Bridgefoot Street, where Massey Brothers, the undertakers, are now. Sometimes my mother sent me to Prescott's the cleaners in Cornmarket. Frawley's and Duffy's were the two big shops of Thomas Street at this time. Thomas Street and High Street together had formed the principal Dublin thoroughfare of the 1700s. They were

Mike Nolan, the well-known Comedian of the Forties and Fifties.

Nicholas Street, looking north to Christ Church (1914).

Looking south from Christ Church into Nicholas Street, High Street to the right.

ousted by Capel Street when Essex Bridge was built, and when Carlisle Bridge i.e. O'Connell Bridge appeared, O'Connell Street took over the premier role.

The old shops of over fifty years ago had a character about them, which the present streamlined version lacks. The shopkeeper knew his customers by their first names and most purchases ended with the phrase 'Put it in the book, please.' One facet of boyhood, which I actually miss, is the weighing of butter. I was sent for, maybe a quarter of butter, that is, four ounces. Mr. Murphy took up two big wooden platters, dipped them in water, sliced a portion of butter from the 56 lb. lump with one platter, and then placed the butter on the scales, with a piece of tissue paper underneath. If too light he added an extra piece; if too heavy he dug out a piece with one platter. When the correct weight was registered, he slapped the piece of butter with the two platters sending drops of water in every direction; then, when the butter was a regular shape, he slipped it into a bag and the act was over.

The 56 lb. butter-boxes were much sought after. Many women made them into low seats with cushioned tops. The boxes were very strongly made, and I am sure that some of them are still in existence. Mrs. Cullen in Haymarket never sold butter.

Like all children, we were keen to go on messages for other people besides our parents. The reason for this keenness was the prospect of a penny or a ha'penny. I went on messages to Cullen's and the Cork Dairy for the Misses Weir, two sisters, who lived at the top of No. 9 in Haymarket. However, there was another way in which we earned money, unknown to our parents. Many of the men who went into the pubs left horses and carts outside. They were always glad when small boys like Tony or Paddy Stynes or myself offered to mind and watch them. To do this, we held the bridle and stood beside the horse. The only snag to this operation was that some of the men forgot to come out and we often went home without payment.

We used the same formula for men with bikes, but most of these ignored us or told us to clear off. Minding the horses was our preference of course, because one had a feeling of being grown-up, when in charge of an animal. We used all the usual expressions that went with the job. 'Hike there, will you! Whoa! Back, back!'

One particular day, it was during the Easter holidays, I was given the task of minding a young mare and trap. The owner went into Minogue's pub and was in no hurry to come out, it seemed. Evidently, the young mare thought the same as myself and she began to move towards the door on the corner. I tried hard to pull her back, but it was no use; she was too strong for me. Eventually she ended up with the front half of her body inside the pub, and the trap and the other half outside. I forgot about my penny reward and ran away. What happened afterwards I never heard.

On another occasion a man with a horse and dray asked Tony Mangan and myself to watch the animal while he was in St. John's pub. After a while, and as the horse seemed a quiet one, we both got up on the dray. I put my feet through the trap-door in the centre and pretended to drive the horse. He must have taken it for the real thing, because he moved off with Tony and myself pulling frantically at the reins. He, however, ignored us completely and ambled down Queen Street and into Benburb Street. Both of us jumped down, ran back to the pub, opened the door and shouted, 'Hey, mister, your horse is headin' for the Phoenix Park.' Then we ran.

Although Tony Mangan's father's shop was the nearest barber's to our house, my mother always sent Mossy and myself to McDonagh's on Ellis Quay. This was a small shop with ten chairs lining two sides of it. On the chairs was a pile of torn worn-out comic-cuts, which I had read a number of times. Outside of the open door one could hear and see the squealing and wheeling seagulls in the Liffey.

'Just a little bit off the back an' sides, me mother says, Mr. McDonagh.'

'How is your mother?'

'Very well, thanks; me father sez he's goin' to get a motor-car.'

'That's great news; I hope you'll give me a jaunt in it. Will you tell your mother that your hair-cut will be going up to fourpence next time.'

'You can tell me father that; he'll be in tonight for a hair-cut. I heard him tellin' me mother.'

'That's fine, and there's a ha'penny for yourself.'

'Thanks very much, Mr. McDonagh.'

The shop had a strong aroma of cheap Brilliantine — it cost
2d. per bottle. We were always sent for our hair-cuts during
the day, because between six o'clock and eight the men were
taken before boys. Most of the men came in for a shave and
Mr. McDonagh used to open on Sunday mornings for special
customers. It was a mystery to me why men went to a barber
for a shave; my father always shaved himself with an open
razor, and always sang while stropping it. Shaving at home, to
me, at any rate, was a happy affair.

I often wondered about the spitoon in the corner of Mr.
McDonagh's shop — these were seen in pubs only — until
one day, I saw a man turn his head as he sat in the chair
and spit right across the room into it. He seemed to be
chewing tobacco, while the barber worked on his head.

The majority of customers asked for a 'back and sides' job,
but now and again one heard, 'I think you can take a little
bit off the top while you're at it.' When the door of the shop
was shut, as was done on wet days, the constant clicking of
the scissors was a very soothing sound. The scissors kept
clicking, even when not actually in contact with the hair.
After the cutting, the hair was liberally doused with oil and
the customer left the shop with a well-plastered coif.
'Th'ould mot likes me hair to look well.'

16 Things My Father Did

Scarcity of meat — Tripe and blind stew — Coddle and 'squint' — Music Hall — The horse in the Tivoli — Power and Bendon — Parties — 'Soup, soup, soup' — The Scholarship — The first radio — Model T IX186 — Bird-breeding — Bicycles.

DURING THE FIRST World War there was very little meat to be had. My father got a rabbit now and again from Wexford. Sausages were the most popular form of meat for a short period after the war. In the early Twenties my mother often bought tripe, which was cheap, and to this day, tripe and onions is one of my favourites. In many homes, a coddle was a popular dish; Mossy liked this but I never did. Butter was dear, so many people used margarine. Stew was popular; I remember my mother telling me to eat up my 'blind stew'. This was stew with no meat. 'Eat up, you'll be followin' a crow for that before Saturday.'

Potatoes and some vegetables seem to have been plentiful enough. During the war, eggs were sevenpence each, while after· the war they were sixpence and eightpence per dozen. I can only remember these things in retrospect; as a young boy I did not pay much attention to the price of food; there was always something on the table when I came in at meal-times, and I don't think that I ever refused anything, even a coddle. There was another meal called Squint — this was composed of new potatoes dipped in milk, which had plenty of salt and peper thrown on. The porridge we ate was made of Indian Meal or Yalla Male as it was called. Another name for it was Burgoo.

My father, as I mentioned before, had made quite a name for himself in Wexford as a comedian and singer, and had always been attracted to the stage. My mother frowned on it and so he performed only at hooleys and parties, where he

155

Martin Crosbie (senior) in hard hat, with two friends, about 1904.

was in great demand. However, every chance my father got, he brought either Mossy or myself to the Tivoli, or Queens, or Royal. This was done often under the pretext of bringing us for a walk. I remember one funny incident which took place in 1923. We, my father and I, had reached the Custom House on our 'walk', when we veered across the Liffey to the Tivoli, now the Irish Press offices. We were late, the last in, in fact, and had to stand at the back of the Parterre. I was able to look up along the centre passage, while my father leaned on the balustrade. A yodeller had finished — it was my first time to hear one — and for the next item a man came out on the stage on a horse, in full hunting gear and commenced to sing 'D'ye Ken John Peel'. After singing one verse, the horse, for no apparent reason, began to walk forward towards the audience. The singer pulled frantically at the reins, but was unable to stop him, and horse and man fell down into the orchestra pit. The laughing that followed I shall always remember. My father, who had a rather high, infectious laugh went into convulsions, and was actually crying with the laughing. After some time the laughing eased and then broke out afresh, helped on by my father. This happened a few times and it was about twenty minutes later that the next turn appeared on the stage. We never heard, for sure, what happened to the horse and man, but the rest of the show was spoiled by spasmodic outbursts of cackling during the night. The Show in the Tivoli ended late on account of this incident, and we missed the last tram home along the quays. As we walked home my father stopped and held every lamp-post, and gave vent to uncontrolled fits of laughing. He told my mother the story, and next day he was laughing still.

My father always went to see Harry Lauder, who was a nice singer, but not much of a comedian. Other names I recall are Albert Burdon, who was very funny, I thought, Shaun Glenville and Dorothy Ward, Madge Clifton, who made a name as a Principal Boy, Power and Bendon, comedians in the Queens and G. H. Elliott, the Chocolate-Coloured Coon.

On some Friday nights my father and mother went out either to the pictures or to a theatre, leaving Mossy in charge of the house. My sister, Mona, always took advantage of such a night to make her own brand of toffee. I can't remember how she made it, because I was interested only in the finished article. She used butter and sugar, I think, and made it on the hob of the range. It always tasted delicious.

On such occasions, we brought in our friends. Mona had Kathleen Atkinson in a few times. Her mother had a Catholic repository in Mary's Lane and Mona had become friendly with her in George's Hill Convent. Another girl who was a great friend of my sister was Maisie Lyons from Haymarket. Mossy had George Kane in on occasions and I had Tony Mangan. I am writing now about the early Twenties.

We had quite a number of parties in our house of course. My father loved company, singing and telling stories. We were put to bed, but we crept down and listened on the stairs to the laughing and clinking of cups and bottles. Our aunts and uncles came to these parties plus some great friends of my parents, like the Malones from Phibsboro' and the Rothwells from Dolphin's Barn. The songs they sang were the old drawing-room type, like 'There is a Flower that Bloometh' and 'When Other Lips'. My father always livened it up with a few comic songs. One song was a quick tongue-twister type of doggerel that went:

'Once I went to Colney Hatch,
  Saw a lovely batch,
  Of people off their thatch.
  One bloke sittin' on a bed
  Told me he was dead.'

In later years I was to learn that Colney Hatch was an asylum in England for mental patients. There was another song which was as old as the hills, I should say, and must have come via the English Music Halls in the Nineties.

'One Christmas I was out of work
    and hadn't got a bob,
  I walked the boots clean off my feet
    now lookin' for a job.
  I took a stroll round Pimlico,
    as I had lots of time,
  And I stopped to read the bills
    about the Christmas Pantomime.

The old Tivoli (1915) (now Irish Press offices).

I saw they wanted some young lads
    to go upon the stage,
And as I had some vacant days
    I thought I would engage;
I went and saw the manager,
    he said I looked all right
And he booked me as a "Super",
    at eighteen d. per night.

Chorus:
Oh they dressed me up in armour,
And they made me look a guy,
They gave me a bang on the top of the conk,
That nearly made me cry,
And they banged me with the bladder,
Till with pain I couldn't stoop,
And the boys upon the gallery shouted
Soup! Soup! Soup!

I asked them where they kept the soup,
    they said they'd like a plate
The manager only laughed and said,
    "Why actors never ate"
And I thought that that's the reason,
    why all actors look so thin,
Sure, you really wouldn't hurt them
    if you pricked them with a pin.
                Repeat Chorus.

The humour of these old songs would leave a present-day audience cold, but the comic song was what an old-time comedian relied on.

My father sang many, many songs at these parties, his favourites being among the compositions of Stephen Foster. He had a beautiful tenor voice and there were always shouts of 'Give us another, Martin' after every song. One song he always sang was 'Jeannie with the Light Brown Hair'.

My father was made an overseer in 1923 and life improved in many ways. He managed to buy a car the following year, a secondhand Model T, which he used for going in and out to Skerries, where he and two others ran dances. The band was one led by Billy Withers, who was very popular at the time.

My father and mother did a complete overhaul of the car. The registration number was IX 186, and its appearance got a great lift from my mother with some beige paint. She also did a job on the hood, which was collapsible, and she repaired the celluloid windshields at the sides. My father had it registered as a hackney. The petrol was 10d. a gallon, there was no insurance and the road tax was £1 as a hackney.

A journey to Wexford town to visit my father's mother took six hours. We had to bring our petrol with us in two gallon tins, as there were no filling stations on the roads. Stopping at Gorey to ask the way, I can still recall the big Wexfordman say 'Keep to the steam-rowled tarry road to Castlebrudge'. In Wexford town small boys were running on both sides of the car as automobiles were not yet a common sight. We met very few cars on the journey.

My father was very fond of birds and used to breed canaries. The terms Yorkshire and Roller come back to me now. I liked the Roller canary myself: his type of singing was called rolling, and it sounded as if the bird had a small marble in its throat while singing. My father went off a few times with a man called Pa Boland to Kinnegad to catch birds. They used lime and I think it was very cruel. However, it was the 'done' thing.

He often went to the Bird Market in Bride Street. The birds bought there, and which he brought home in a paper bag, only lived a couple of days. The story was that as the seller was handing the finch or linnet to the buyer he gave the bird a gentle squeeze. The bird would die on Tuesday and the man would return on the following Sunday. I believed this story then.

There were many people in Dublin interested in birds. Bird-cages were to be seen hanging from nails outside of the windows of the tenement houses. Maybe they reminded country people of the green fields at home; the birds certainly sang in their cages.

Although money was 'as scarce as hobby-horse manure', my father managed to produce a bicycle for the three of us, Mossy, Mona and myself. We took our turns using the bike, which was a girl's model, a Pierce, noted for its strength and durability. I got the bike every Monday and Thursday, plus

161

Bird cages on wall of Dublin's slimmest house (Winetavern Street).

every third Sunday. The year was 1924 and I think the bicycle cost fifteen shillings. It had to be a lady's model, of course.

My father also brought home a carbide lamp, a type of lamp which was reputed to be dangerous and liable to explode. The first chance I got, one dark night, after tea, I set the carbide lamp and rode the bicycle up along the lonely Main Road of the Phoenix Park as far as the Eagle Monument — this monument was out in the middle of the road at this time — just for the sheer joy of seeing the flickering light on the dark road in front of me. The British had gone at this time and curfew days were over.

Mossy and I were careful with that bike and I often gave jaunts to my pals. Each boy sat on the saddle, while I stood on the pedals and pushed.

There was one great test which had to be undergone by the owner of a bike. It entailed cycling out to Chapelizod, pushing the bike to the top of Glenmaroon Hill under and beyond the connecting bridge and then free-wheeling down the hill *without touching the brakes.* This took some doing and if you don't believe me, I invite you to have a go.

The bicycle also brought us quite often to a place of happy memories; it was Knockmaroon and the Strawberry Beds near the Wren's Nest. The Wren's Nest was an old, dilapidated pub on the right hand side; our destination was the old ruined mill opposite. There was a weir here and from 1925 onwards, I went on outings there with different companions. It was also a very popular spot for picking blackberries. The outings from Queen Street used to halt at the Strawberry Hall. The revellers danced on the roadway in front of the hall.

> It is often that my memory
> Brings me down the road of dreams,
> To the dear old Liffey Valley,
> And my own dear boyhood scenes,
> Where we played and swam and quarrelled,
> Where the hours passed all too soon;
> Oh, God be with those boyhood days,
> And with you, sweet Knockmaroon

Thatched tea-rooms at the Strawberry Hall.

I can see the blossomed orchards,
Where the Liffey flows along,
Where the fisherman sits quietly
And the blackbird sings his song . . .
And the trees we went a-climbing
In those warm sweet days of June,
Those were the days we loved the best,
In the fields at Knockmaroon.

(Recorded by Martin Crosbie, Written by Paddy.)

Dublin became full of bicycles during the late Twenties. I graduated in 1926 from the girl's bike to a semi-racer fixed-wheel, which Mossy and I shared. My father bought it from one of John Murray's racing friends. I became so proficient in the use of the fixed wheel, that I was able to bring the bike to a dead stop — no mean feat, if you appreciate what a fixed-wheel bike really was.

Whenever anything went wrong with the bike, either Mossy or myself headed for Abbey Street Upper to two shops, one with the name O'Connor over the window, the other with the name O'Malley. If O'Connor hadn't the required part one was sent next-door to O'Malley and vice versa. I am sure every cyclist in Dublin visited these two shops. They were situated a mere few steps from the corner of Capel Street. The site is now a car-park.

The fixed-wheel bicycle lasted up to the end of the Twenties. I can't remember the last time I used it; it just disappeared from our lives. What happened to it, I do not know, but while my brother and I had it in our possession we got full value from it.

Another popular, homemade, street vehicle was the box-car. There were four wheels, usually wheels taken from old skates. The front axle swivelled from the front centre and the steering was done with a rope tied to the axle on the inner side of the front wheels. These had to be pushed, but we brought them to the hills at Grangegorman or Constitution Hill, where no pushing was needed.

Scooters were popular. My father made Mossy and myself two very good ones, which we used when going on messages. The best place for scooters was the path on the south-east of Smithfield, leading down to the corner of Phoenix Street.

The year was 1925.

1926 was an important year for me as it was the year I was awarded a Corporation Scholarship, but it was an important year for everybody else in Ireland too. On January 1, Radio Éireann was launched from the big tall red building in Denmark Street (it was demolished in 1978) and the whole world was talking about this new miracle. The programmes appeared in the papers — information which was useless unless one had a receiving set. The Irish station was called 2.R.N.

The first time I ever listened in was early in 1926 at the home of Paul Butterly on Richmond Road. My father brought me with him and when the earphones were put on I was amazed to hear a man singing. I think his name was Cathal McGarvey.

In the meantime, everyone was making his own set. The parts were available for one and ninepence in Woolworths — the principal part being a small cylinder-shaped glass with the crystal inside, plus a catswhisker which was prodded into the crystal until a good spot was found. Of course there was a snag — one needed earphones. The crystal itself was like a tiny piece of coal or coke. I soon had a set of my own, but we had only one pair of headphones. My father had paid seven shillings and sixpence for them. Soon after this he began talking about buying a gramophone.

17 The Trams of Old Dublin

First tram 1896 (Electric) — The luxury tram to Dalkey — Steam trams — The Piano-stool — 'Massa Bones' — Nelson Pillar — Blessington 1924 — Howth Tram — Tower Buses — Lucan Tram — The 'Dirt' tram — Open-tops.

THE ELECTRIC TRAMS were a feature of my young days. Horse-drawn trams commenced operations between College Green and Rathgar in 1872 and the system spread quickly. The electric trams made their appearance in 1896. The last Dublin tram made its final journey in 1949 to Dalkey. Most trams were four-wheeled, but the larger trams on the Dalkey, Howth and Lucan routes were eight wheelers. There were different types of trams also, the open top, the covered top with balcony ends, the completely covered saloons and finally the luxury tram on the Dalkey line. My father played a part in the making of this luxury tram and his photograph appeared in the newspapers with the others involved. The picture was taken in the tram itself; the principals involved were a Mr. Malone and a Mr. Courtney.

The Dublin and Blessington, and Hill of Howth tramways, never came under the control of the Dublin United Tramway Co. The steam tram to Blessington operated up to the year 1932; the Hill of Howth tram lasted until 1959. One thing all of my generation can claim — we never had to wait very long for a tram. The service was non-stop, most unlike the bus-service.

We all loved the trams. There was no other way of getting around, of course, and the parallel lines of tracks were to be seen on every main thoroughfare. As boys we made use of these tracks by putting ha'pennies on them when we had them. These were transformed into pennies by the passing trams, and were often used for the Penny Rush at the Feeno when Morrissy at the door had no time for scrutinising coins, as we slapped them down on the table.

My father, being an employee of the Dublin United Tramway Company, had a free pass, and he was well-known to all of the conductors and drivers on the quay run. Our usual tram into town was the No. 24, which we boarded outside of Lynch's tailoring shop on Arran Quay. As soon as we got on the tram — by we, I mean the family this time — I always made a dash for the 'piano-stool'. This was a movable round-topped seat, which screwed into the floor of the sliding doors at each end of the tram. It was changed from one end to the other in the 'downstairs' section of the tram. My father explained that it was placed in front of one of the doors, to prevent passengers from leaving the tram by the wrong exit, after the tram had stopped at a terminus.

There was a particular, jolly individual whom we met on the No. 24 a few times. He took over the piano-stool and assuming the pose of Massa Johnson in a minstrel show, began addressing passengers on each side as Bones and Rastus. He had the whole tram in good humour and my father really enjoyed him, because he himself had been a member of a minstrel group in Wexford town.

'Mister Bones, I heard your wife is not lookin' well.'

'Yassah, Massa Johnson, mah wife ain't lookin' too well — she never looked well — in fact she looks downright ugly.'

The numbers 23 and 24 ran along the north quays; the former was a ten minute service, the latter a three minute one. The number 22 ran on the south quays and its destination was Rathmines. This service however, did not run on Sundays. I learned these details from my father, who could answer any questions on the subject of trams. Most tram services started from Nelson Pillar, which naturally became the centre of the universe, as far as Dubliners were concerned. 'I'll meet you at the Pillar at seven.'

The family went to Blessington on St. Patrick's Day 1923 on the steam tram. First we took the ordinary tram No. 16 to Terenure and there we boarded the steam tram. In effect, it was very much like a train and the clickety-clack sound of the wheels on the tracks emphasised the similarity. There were two carriages and these were open at the sides. Both

Martin Crosbie (senior) standing (in hard hat) in the first luxury tram to Dalkey.

carriages were roofed. It was a rather slow chug-chug journey on the way out, as it was ninety per cent uphill. The journey back was different; we came flying along on the tracks at a tremendous speed and my mother was ever so nervous. The tracks lay close to the right-hand side on the way down, and it was no wonder that there had been many deaths of people coming out directly onto the trackway from their front gates. When we arrived at the Terenure terminus there was a large crowd waiting to take our places.

On the other side of the city we had numbers 30 and 31, which brought us to Dollymount and Howth. We travelled on two occasions up to the Hill of Howth. Fairview Park was the sloblands at this time, and was not a very beautiful sight going or coming. In fact, when anyone wished to describe a bad smell the expression was 'It was like the old sloblands'.

The tram tracks themselves were always a great hazard to cyclists. The groove of the rail seemed to be the exact width of a bicycle tyre (which by the way, was always 28 x 1½) and one had to be very careful to cross the tracks at a good angle. Anything approaching a parallel movement spelt disaster.

The first buses that I remember were the 'Tower' buses, which plied between Parkgate Street and Lucan. These buses started from the big hoarding in Parkgate Street. The colour was green and there was always a heavy smell of oil and petrol in or near them. The fare to Lucan was 4d. These buses were run in opposition to the electric trams of the D.U.T. Co. They rattled a good deal and the journey was a very bumpy one. The electric tram to Lucan ran on the right-hand side of the Conyngham Road, but crossed the road beyond Islandbridge.

Lucan was a very popular place, of course, and a great favourite with Dubliners. The Sarsfield Demesne was the big attraction, where there was swimming and boating for all. The catch-phrase of the Twenties was 'Lucan looks lovely' and the title was well deserved. On Sundays, the Lucan trams were jammed with people.

The 'dirt tram' of Dublin Corporation used come up from the quays along Queen Street, and through George's Lane, on its way to Stanley Street, which is off North Brunswick Street. Stanley Street is (I think) the only place in the city, where old tram-tracks may still be seen. Many of the old trams had open tops, that is, there was no protection from the weather. The backs of the wooden seats were reversible, so that one could choose to face forward or backward. All of the Ballybough trams were open-topped. Small boys loved the open-topped trams. We were able to shout at passers-by. Passing a standing horse, as the animal relieved itself on the roadway, the chorus went up, 'Hey, mister, your horse is losing his petrol!'

> 'The conductor took our fares then
> And each boy gave a "wing".
> He gave us each a ticket
> And his bell went ting-a-ling.
> But when he came to Hobby,
> His money for to take,
> Poor Hobby searched his pockets —
> Sure, he hadn't got a "make".

Trams outside of the R.D.S. 1919.

18 The School Around the Corner

Monitors — The Hail Mary — The Brothers — Kevin Barry is captured — Nicknames — School-caps — Honesty the best policy — Brother Murray and Bill Small — The history bug — School fees — Sunday Catechism — Mr. Kinshella — Eddie Hewitt and the grenade — Manual — Brunner Blunders — Brother Stone and Brother Brick.

The School Around the Corner's still the same
The School that taught you how to play the game
It hasn't changed at all,
That old table's in the hall
Although the master's older, and he's lame.

You left there long ago to make your name,
And we know you'll never, never bring it shame;
You didn't learn so much,
But that old school left its touch,
Yes, the School Around the Corner's still the same.

Not complete. Full song published by Waltons 1951.
Words and music by P. Crosbie.

I ARRIVED AT the Christian Brothers' School, North Brunswick Street, on August 23rd, 1920. The old school was, and still is, a solid building. In 1920 there was only one main building, with a science room and a manual room at the rear. The school has always been called Brunner.

The main building began its life in February, 1869, ten years before the apparitions at Knock. The walls are of Wicklow granite and I believe this old building will be standing, when all the new ones at present surrounding it, have

172

Paddy and the School Around the Corner, St. Paul's CBS, Nth. Brunswick Street.

fallen. There were four very large rooms, each of which was given the title of School. A boy commenced in First School and finished upstairs in Fourth School.

When I arrived from Stanhope Street Convent at the age of six and three-quarters, Brother Curley was examining the newcomers in the Second Reader. I passed with flying colours because I had most of the lessons off by heart from watching and listening to my brother Mossy. Brother Curley had succeeded Brother Redmond, who had earned a great name for saintliness.

When Brunner opened its doors first in February 1869, according to the annals, practically all of the boys who turned up to be enrolled were barefooted. They were an unruly lot, as none had ever been to school before. Beside the school was a site, lately vacated by the Medical School, and when the boys were let out to play, they made their way to this site, where, within a large shed, they found human bones. One of the Brothers was horrified to find his new pupils playing hurling with the skulls and bones. He quickly took command and the bones were interred in a safe place.

The cost of the original building was £4,000. The Brothers were made welcome in the district, and lived for a while in Prussia Street, before removing to the corner of Charleville Road on the North Circular Road. The present monastery is on the other side of the N.C. Road at No. 242.

The desks in First School were long wooden affairs and very shaky. One shake from a boy at one end put blots on twelve copies. The inkwells were filled with a home-made black concoction, and the ink was used for more purposes than writing. There was no formal teaching done, as we know it now, simply because the room was too crowded. There were three monitors and one brother. His name was Brother Cass, and he had succeeded a Brother Morrissy. The monitors were 'five bob a week' ex-pupils, whose job it was to examine the boys in home tasks. The tasks were allotted each afternoon for home-work, and these were examined the following morning. The names of the monitors in First School in 1920 were Lawless, Caffrey and Fitzsimons. We had no fully qualified lay teachers. A failure at lessons meant a chalk-mark on the desk in front of the boy who failed. For every chalk-mark a scholar received one 'biff' from the Brother, but we always managed to lighten our troubles by rubbing out some of the marks before his tour began. Brother Cass used a leather, which we all preferred to the sticks used by the monitors when the brother left the room.

The schoolyard was a very small one — too small for almost six hundred boys. There was no lighting or heating in the rooms, although there was a stove for the latter purpose — a stove which was never used. There were no cloakrooms, so coats and caps were hung on hooks on three walls of each room. Along the fourth wall, which was a wood-plus-glass partition affair, there was a rostrum for the Brother and a large altar to the Blessed Virgin with presses beneath. Every time the clock struck the classes stood and recited a Hail Mary and in the month of May the wooden structure of the altar was covered and decorated with blue and white paper. The boys brought in flowers and candles, and there was great rivalry between the classrooms, as to which altar was the best.

The lavatories in the schoolyard were dry ones, but were flushed periodically by a mysterious someone, whom we never saw. Later on in 1924 Brother Murray had the old toilets knocked down and a line of twelve new flush ones plus a wash-hand basin and urinals built on a new extension of the schoolyard. Civilization had arrived.

Long before the British left Ireland the Christian Brothers were teaching Irish. The Brothers used a huge chart of pictures for conversation lessons, and their 'Aids to Irish Composition' was a book which gave wonderful help in problems of grammar. I doubt that it will ever be bettered. Regarding the chart, I can recall every figure and scene on it.

As I entered the school in 1920, I little dreamed that I was destined to spend almost fifty-seven years of my life within its confines, or that my own name was to be wedded to that of the school that was to become 'The School Around the Corner'.

Brother Hoolahan was in charge of Second School; Brother Doyle was upstairs in Third School. He was to be succeeded by Brother Ryan by the time I reached that height. Brother Donovan was in charge of Fourth School. Brother Hoolahan I liked very much; he it was, who gave me an interest in history, particularly local history, which I mention elsewhere.

It was he who taught us:

> 'Did they dare? Did they dare?
> To slay Owen Roe O'Neill?
> Yes, they slew him with poison
> They feared to meet with steel.'

I was only four weeks in Brunner when, one Monday morning, we heard shots. It was about half-eleven. Brother Curley shut the school gates, but as soon as we got the chance, we all raced down Brunswick Street to the corner, about 150 yards, to hear for the first time, how a lad named Kevin Barry had been captured by the British. Two soldiers were killed. A British lorry, with soldiers had come down Constitution Hill to collect bread rations at Monk's Bakery and had been ambushed. I heard that Kevin Barry had intended to sit an examination in the university at 2 p.m. that day. On November 1st, 1920, the morning of his execution, after waiting outside Mountjoy Jail with the crowds my mother left Mossy and myself at my grandmother's. Everybody was talking about Kevin Barry and Terence MacSwiney at this time. I think the song 'Kevin Barry' was being sung on the Dublin Streets that very night. The Brothers taught us the words later.

> 'In Mountjoy Jail one Monday morning,
> High upon the gallows tree
> Kevin Barry gave his young life,
> For the cause of liberty.'

Near our school, at the corner of Red Cow Lane stood a sweet-shop, Donohue's, where we got a fistful of white lozenges for a penny, or for the same amount, a large hunk of a very popular eatable, named 'Paralysed Puddin'. Mrs. Donohue did not resent the name. The school itself faces the old Richmond Hospital, now St. Laurence's, and I can remember a huge funeral from the hospital in the mid-Twenties. A few years later the name of the man who died, was to crop up in our studies — Pádraig Ó Conaire.

We got half-an-hour for lunch, and, during the thirty minutes, we ran, or scutted home, gulped down a dinner and got back before the bell rang at one o'clock. On Thursdays, there was always a possibility of being late as quite often we stopped to watch a tinkers' fight in Smithfield near Red Cow Lane.

School fights were always settled 'up the lane'. I remember still the great fight between McCarthy and Fannin. School concerts were a regular feature at the break-up for holidays, and I recall the songs sung by one particular boy. His name was Paddy Tyrrell, and it was no surprise to us to hear that he became a professional comedian, one of the famous Happy Gang. One of his songs went:

'I took Miss McNally for to see a Fancy Ball
The tickets they were three and six and my money was
   rather small
And when she asked for supper, sure she nearly
   knocked me down
For all the money I had in the world was only a
   half-a-crown.'

There were many colourful characters in Brunner, and an amazing collection of nicknames to go with them. There was Boxer Foley, Darkie Sullivan, Snowball Balfe, Harrier Devine, Muttoner Dunn, Hobby Dunn, Whacker Moore, Whacker Dowdall, Gero, Mousey Ryan, Snodser Quinn, the two Harros, Giant Brennan, Chicken Byrne, Glaxo Gorman, Snub Bollard, Mucky Maher (who came from St. Gabriel's to join our hurling team), Yeemo Gaffey, Dough Callan, Leadner Murphy, Mary O'Brien, Parky Ryan, Steve Donohue, Tiger Lyons, Eyebrows O'Brien, Puddener O'Brien, Ramsey McDonnell, etc. I hope all of the above will forgive me for resurrecting their schoolday nicknames. The teachers did not escape and old Brunnerites will remember Lannylegs, Chenty, Juicy and Napoleon. The boys played tricks on Chenty and gave him ridiculous answers. One day, when Peadar Clifford was absent, Paddy O'Brien (whom we called Mary), who had been told to tell the Master that Peadar had ring-worm, told Chenty instead that he had woodworm in his head. Another day he asked Seán Moore 'When should a cow be milked?' The answer he got was 'Every morning and every evening and in all dangers, temptations and afflictions'. However, nobody played tricks on Napoleon, who was Brother Declan Ryan. He made everybody work, and there was no way of dodging him. But the man who 'made' the school, the man who set the school on an upward trend was Brother Murray, who succeeded Brother Curley as Superior.

Formal teaching was just not feasible, on account of the

Some of the famous Happy Gang Queen's Theatre — Frankie Howerd, Mick Eustace, Gloria Greene, Paddy Tyrrell (holding Evening Mail), Bill Brady, Freddie Doyle, Cecil Nash.

numbers and the presence of two — sometimes three — teachers in the one room. The teacher with the stronger voice always won. The general method of teaching was hit and run; if a boy didn't pay attention, he was left behind. The Brothers had to fall back on memorisation; this suited some of the pupils.

The boys in Brunner wore special maroon-coloured caps — it was the custom in all Christian Brothers' Schools to wear caps. On our caps were the interwoven capital letters B.C.N.S. signifying Christian Brothers' School, North Brunswick Street. However, when I got mine, I was told that the real meaning of the letters was Brother Curley Never Slaps. And, of course, Brother Curley did slap.

Besides our lunch or dinner break at 12.30 p.m., there was a short interval at 10.30 a.m., when we were all let loose in the small yard. Whenever an accident occurred in the playground, the injured boy was sent over to the Richmond Hospital opposite the school, where eager students made mountains out of mole-hills. A boy with a cut finger came back with his arm in a sling. However, everybody was pleased to have such a first aid so near.

The Brothers had no finesse about dishonesty. Everything was in black and white. One day a boy — now a prominent and respected citizen — was discovered with a fountain pen belonging to another pupil. He admitted the theft and was expelled. The actual expulsion was a physical, visible one and we, the pupils, were allowed to crowd the windows and the exit from the yard to watch the scene. The 'thief' was brought to the front gate by Brother Murray, gripped by the collar of the coat and the seat of his pants, and heaved out onto the roadway. His schoolbag was thrown after him plus his cap. Then the Brother, dusting his hands symbolically, gave the signal to return to our classes. That punishment was very rough and very severe indeed, but during the Twenties there was no pilfering or dishonesty in our school, directly as a result of that vivid expulsion. Another thing, there was no such thing as impertinence and 'yessir' in all conversation with teachers signified a respect for authority.

'William Dunn, were you in school yesterday?'
'No!'
'No, what?'

Paddy Crosbie, centre back, with classmates (1926).

'No boots, sir.'

Whatever the reason, and I feel respect for authority in school and at home was ninety per cent of it, there was little or no vandalism during the so-called turbulent Twenties.

Brother Murray was a real live-wire. He brought us to factories, the museum and historical places. He prepared us for scholarships like a trainer preparing a fighter for a championship bout, and when he finally left the school, he left a trail of scholarship holders behind him, some of whom forgot to thank him. He died in 1974 at the age of ninety-four. I could never have repaid my debt to him. To me, he was the Daddy of all Christian Brothers.

In the Twenties the hurling teams of Brunner were second to none in the City of Dublin. This was due to the coaching of Bill Small, himself an All-Ireland gold medallist. We feared him in school and he made us develop a do-or-die spirit that boded ill for other schools. O'Connell Schools were our greatest rivals. On one occasion, we were due to play O'Connell's in the Final in the Fifteen Acres. On the morning of the match, Thursday, our star player, Seán Moore, was absent from school. Bill Small nearly had a fit. He sent a boy up to Seán's house in Cowper Street and received this reassuring note from Mrs. Moore. 'Dear Mr. Small, Seán is sick and cannot go to school today, but he will most certainly be up for the Final in the Park this afternoon, Mrs. Moore.' In the years 1923, 1924 and 1925 many boys from Brunner used to attend Irish classes in 39 Parnell Square. This was done on the direction of Brother Murray. In the beginning, we made fun of the whole scheme:

'Taw shay mahogany gas-pipes
Ock neel shay, taw shay muck the full of a hand-cart.'

One thing we did learn was Irish songs, which we used to sing on the way home along Bolton Street and North King Street.

Sometimes, we attended Irish classes in Colmcille Hall in Blackhall Street. The teacher was Seán O h-Aodha, whom we called Johnnie O'Straw. The Colmcille Hall was the same hall, where the Irish Volunteers had mustered on Easter Monday in 1916. Part of the wall of Newgate Prison was used in building the basement of the hall. Before 1916 this Hall was the meeting place for all those associated with the freedom movement and drilling with hurleys was carried on in the big room.

But I am travelling too fast and must go back to Second School and Brother Hoolahan. When I began to learn about Irish History I took a great interest in historical spots. I remember making my way to Thomas Street and standing outside the line of houses facing the Public Library, wondering as to which of these houses Robert Emmet had used as his depot. I walked around to the rear — by Marshalsea Lane to Marshal Lane — it was still a lane at this time — for the same purpose. I saw in my mind's eye Emmet and his men moving out into Bridgefoot Street (Dirty Lane) on that Saturday in July and turning up and into Thomas Street. 'Bould Robert Emmet, the darlin' of Erin.' I roamed around the old Marshalsea Barracks. The steps inside were of stone and the entire place seemed cold and unfriendly. The courtyard was cobbled. The Library in Thomas Street is built on the site of a house used as a hide-out by Lord Edward Fitzgerald. He was captured, of course, in Nicholas Murphy's on the opposite side, Number 151. When Brother Hoolahan gave us details about Wolfe Tone, I made my own way to Stafford Street and although his birthplace is claimed to be situated at the south end of the street I remember distinctly standing outside a tenement house about four doors from Parnell Street and noting a plaque on the wall concerning Tone's birth in 1763. I learned also that his mother and father first lived in South Earl Street, off Meath Street, before settling in Stafford Street.

I stood at the south-east corner of the Esplanade at Sarsfield Quay and pictured it as the Croppies' Field, when the green field sloped down to the Liffey itself, and when there was no road or wall by the river. Brother Hoolahan told us about all of the Croppies who were buried here, including Wolfe Tone's younger brother. Next on my list was St. Werburgh's Church. It took me a long time to find this place, as nobody else seemed interested.

The Bermingham Tower of Dublin Castle engaged my attention too. This tower held a fascination for me because of the Two Hughs, who were my idols. In Brother Hoolahan's class the Battle of Kinsale became a personal defeat. 'That Don Juan D'Aguila was a dirty lookin' eejit.'

I was an altar boy at this time and Brother Hoolahan let

182

Marshalsea Lane.

me off very often to serve Mass at 10 o'clock. There was a Mr. Murphy in Second School with the brother at this period: I don't think he was a mere monitor.

When I arrived in Brunner the school fees were threepence per week, but in 1924 they were raised to sixpence. Friday was 'school-money' day and the brother spent a harassing two hours collecting the money. How the schools managed to exist on this money is a mystery, especially as so many stood up and said, 'I forgot it, sir.' There were no government grants for the Christian Brothers in the Twenties. Many boys got 'free' education from the Brothers, before it was 'invented'.

One facet of life in a Christian Brothers' School was Catechism on Sunday. This was a compulsory class from 9.30 to 10.30 a.m. Stories from the Bible were read for us, and sometimes the Lives of the Saints were used. Woe betide anyone who stayed away from Catechism on Sunday; he paid for it on Monday. No other schools had this type of Sunday class. However, many liked it as there was no 'Biffing'.

The British Army was stationed in the old North Dublin Union or Workhouse, behind the Richmond Hospital and the Catholic soldiers marched every Sunday to 11 o'clock Mass in the garrison church on Arbour Hill. They always marched to the music of a British Military Band, and as soon as we heard the music, we flew to the windows to look out, because all boys loved a band. The Brother never minded and, anyway, Catechism time was ending.

A funny incident occurred in Brother Hoolahan's class one Monday. It concerned Arthur O'Sullivan, the well-known actor. Arthur was known in schooldays as Archie and lived in Queen Street with his widowed mother. On this particular Monday Archie was kept home and was marked absent. During the morning, Archie's mother sent him for a pint of milk. Archie went with the jug to the dairy in King Street and was reading a comic-cut. Coming out of the shop, instead of turning right, he turned left and continued on, holding the jug of milk with one hand, and the comic-cut with the other. Absent-mindedly he turned into Red Cow Lane, then Brunswick Street, then the school gate, finally the schoolroom door. There was consternation, when Archie walked into the classroom, carrying the jug of milk. As Archie couldn't explain the situation, the laughing went on for quite a while.

The following is the text of an *Irish Independent* newspaper article after Archie's death on 18th February 1981: 'One of Ireland's best-known actors, Arthur (Archie) O'Sullivan, has died aged 69. A Dubliner, he was a member of the RTE Players and appeared in many stage, radio and television productions. His first stage appearance was in the Gaiety Theatre in 1941 when he played in Juno and the Paycock. Regarded as one of the real professionals of the stage, Mr. O'Sullivan spent many years 'on the road' in Irish theatres.'

There was an old man named Mr. Kinshella who lived in a room in Queen Street also. He had a big mop of snow-white hair, and he often sat on one of the buffer stones at the drinking trough in Haymarket. He used to talk to the children and tell us about games he played in Camolin, Co. Wexford, when he was young. One day — it was about 1925 — he discovered that I was interested in historical places and he told me some items of interest that I have never forgotten. He told me that the original plans for St. Patrick's Hospital (now at James's Street) were for the building to be sited at Queen Street. I don't know whether this is true or not; I do remember Mr. Kinshella saying this. He also mentioned that John Mitchel spent his last night, before deportation, in a prison situated at the north east corner of Smithfield. The prison was still there in 1925; it had been a prison for females originally. At the moment the Dublin Corporation have built houses on the site.

I told Brother Hoolahan in Brunner about Mr. Kinshella and one day the old man came along to the school. We learned from Brother Hoolahan that the man from Wexford had been born in the year of the Famine, and that his grandfather had been killed on Vinegar Hill in 1798.

> When the Brother teaches History,
> Each week he picks one day.
> We fold our arms an' sit up straight,
> Our books is pur'away.
> We listen very quietly
> To the stories he does tell,

An' every time the Irish win,
We all ler' out a yell.

I like them History lessons,
'Cause the Brother's not so cross,
He sorta changes inside out,
An' never tries to boss.
He looks a little oldish, now,
But when the History comes,
He seems to get real young again,
Not like when doin' sums.

Brother Hoolahan could be cross at times and I can remember a day, when he broke a pointer on Harrier Devine's head. I suppose the pointer was split at the time, but Brother Hoolahan was a man who would stand for no nonsense. Mr. Murphy, the other teacher, was a rather quiet man, but he never had any trouble from us, because of the brother's presence in the room.

It was about this time that Eddie Hewitt, Mick Conway and Tom King found a grenade and didn't know what it was. Throwing and kicking it around, it exploded and Eddie lost most of the fingers from one hand. After that, we were all warned about the dangers of picking up metal things.

Manual, or carpentry, was taught in Brunner for many years by Brother Maher, a Tipperary man. Nobody disliked Brother Maher. He had a red shining, smiling face, wore glasses, and was very gentle and kind. Every boy was anxious to get into the Manual class; however I was unlucky enough to be left out. The class was held in a special room called the Manual room, which was situated beside the Science Room.

On Thursdays we got a half-day from school. The half-day had to be spent in the Phoenix Park. This was the time of great rivalry between our school and O'Connell Schools. On Saturday afternoons we went hurling after school near the Dog Pond. This was the place where we made the acquaintance of one particular hawker of fruit. He was a small man and I judged him to be an ex-British soldier. He approached us, always chanting a litany of his wares. In no time everybody knew the chant:

'Apples a pound,
Pears a half-pound,
Bananas each a piece,
Take your hands off the barrow,
Here's the polis,
Cleeves Caramels ten a penny,
Funny Wonder or Chips,
News of the Next World,
Are you buyin'?
No? Well, I won't sell.'

All of which had really nothing to do with the apples and oranges, which he sold to us.

Our school, like every school, had its own store of funny answers.

When would you be late for Mass?
When I wouldn't be in time, Father.

Were Adam and Eve married?
No Father, they hadn't the Parish Priest and two witnesses.

What is Faith?
It's a place in Cabra, Father, where my mother won a set of delf. (Fete)

Who was Abraham?
He was President of the United States.

That is not the correct way to bless yourself.
I get mixed up in the shoulders, Father.

What is martyrdom?
When a man and a woman get married.

What is the most necessary thing in Baptism?
A child, Father.

Children are supposed to be here for Confession before 5 p.m.
I had no sins then, Father.

Prize winning bulls with red rosettes —
They must have made their Confirmation.

Can you do Arithmetic?
No, I can do sums.

The Pyramids are between France and Spain.

What is your father?
I think he is a simple servant.

My father's a B.L.
What's that?
A builder's labourer.

What happened on Easter Sunday?
All the Volunteers came to Dublin.

Now I lay me down to sleep
I pray to God my soul to keep
If he hollers let him go,
Eeny, Meeny Miny Mo.

In the Sacrament of the Sick, what oil is used?
Castor oil, Father.

All men will rise again on the last day.
What happens the women, Father?

Why is a baby baptised shortly after being born?
Because if they waited till he was hardy, Father, he'd be too
heavy to carry to the font.

Give me a prayer that your mother says at home!
Oh God grant me patience!

Act of Contrition
Oh my God I am heartily sorry for having no family
(Oh my God I am heartily sorry for having offended thee)

What must you do before you enter the Confessional?
You must examine your tonsils.

What is a bridegroom?
It's a thing that's used at a weddin', Father.

How did God know that Adam and Eve had eaten the apple?
He saw the butt, Father.

If I had a pound of my own I would buy a farm and get married.

Mountjoy is the place you are put, when you're took.

A boy named Billy Byrne used to come over at week-ends to stay with his aunt in Queen Street. He lived in Francis Street and attended the Christian Brothers' School there. We swapped stories about our schools, and when I told him about the initials on our caps meaning Brother Curley Never Slaps, he told me a funny one about the Superior in Francis Street. It was about 1919 and Brother Brick was due to be transferred. Everybody waited for the new man, and who should he turn out to be but Brother Stone. The 'Stone' and 'Brick' bit really tickled all the boys who heard the story.

North Brunswick Street, or Channel Row, was fairly important in the nineteenth century. The Dominican nuns, now in Cabra, were originally in Channel Row from 1717 to 1807 when they had to leave but they arrived back in 1819 from France. The Convent was situated on the site occupied by St. Laurence's Hospital. During my school days the French Sisters of Charity had a convent, St. John's Convent, next to the hospital. The building is still there, and is now part of the Hardwicke Hospital. A three-storey house, which is now one-storeyed and used also by St. Laurence's, and which stood facing Red Cow Lane was said to be Lady Tyrconnell's House around the time of the Battle of the Boyne.

This same building was, in all probability, part of an old Benedictine nunnery. After James II's defeat they left for Flanders. The Poor Clares moved into this same building in

Channel Row in the 1700s, and were succeeded by the Dominicans.

When the Christian Brothers arrived, on the invitation of the Parish Priest of St. Paul's Arran Quay, they built their school on the south side of Brunswick Street. Since 1869 many physical changes in the building have taken place, but, deep down, The School Around the Corner's still the same.

Paddy Crosbie (centre at rear) with school hurling team 1929.

19 Christmas and Pantos

Christmas — Woolworths — Moore Street — Big shops of the Twenties — Christmas Eve — Christmas Day — Father Mathew Hall — Singing to the queues — After Christmas.

CHRISTMAS IN DUBLIN was Christmas no matter what trouble or war was on. During the very poor period up to about 1920, toys were very scarce in all homes. Rag dolls, many of them home-made, and wooden toys like engines, were the usual ones for girls and boys respectively. Stockings were hung up, however, on Christmas Eve, no matter how bleak the outlook.

I got a meccano set, No. 1A, in 1920 that I cherished and kept intact for years. Mona got her first real doll the same year, one with a smooth rosy face and a head of hair. The body was just rag and sawdust. When Mossy and I were altar-boys, Christmas morning was a very busy one as each priest 'said' three Masses. But there was electricity in the air.

The days before Christmas were full of magic. Woolworth's 'the 3d. and 6d. store' was a fairyland to all children and unknown to our parents we — some of the gang and myself — often sneaked down town to wander up and down through the counters in Woolworth's store. We eyed the toys enviously — most of them were German made — and dreamed of stockings full to the top with the toys on show. We paid visits also to a small Bazaar on the other side of Henry Street. There were no fairy lights strung across the street, but the well-lit windows of every shop in Henry Street and Mary Street satisfied us to the full.

Whenever my mother brought the three of us downtown, we visited Todd Burn's, the Henry Street Warehouse (now Roches Stores), Arnott's, Brown Thomas and Clery's. She only did this, when she had something definite in mind,

A busy Earl Street at Christmas.

usually a pair of shoes. She made most of the clothes we wore and often, in my bed, I could hear the whirr of the old Singer Sewing Machine which she pedalled in spasms to complete a pair of trousers, or a jacket, for Mossy or myself.

To us, Moore Street was the heart of Christmas. My father loved to bring us with him through the Christmas throngs and listen to the wit and sarcasm of the hawkers:

'Listen ma'am, if you're not buying, I'll trouble you to stop maulin' that turkey.'

'I have a right to feel the goods, before I decide to buy.'

'Hey, Julia, come over here and listen to this oul' wan. There's chokes-off being gev by her ladyship.'

As I let my mind wander back to the Christmasses of long ago I find myself listing the well known shops of the period. I remember Hopkins & Hopkins, Elvery's, Lemons, McDowells, Findlaters, the Carlisle Building, the name of Albert Coates the piano tuner — all of them in O'Connell Street. In Capel Street, there were Baxendales, McQuillans and Kearneys. In Henry Street besides the Henry Street Warehouse, there were Todd Burns, Liptons, and the Fifty Shilling Tailors. Atkinson's Poplin and Walpole's Irish Linen also come to mind. And from the grown-ups we heard:

'Are yeh goin' home for Christmas?'

'No, I'm sendin' a pound instead.'

I can't remember any Santa Clauses in the shops in those early days. Maybe they were there, but I don't remember being brought to see one. One thing I can remember clearly is the three consecutive Christmas Eves when my father came home drunk with the same friend, Paul Butterly, each carrying a large turkey. On the three occasions my father did the very same thing — he got sick and then fell asleep on the sofa in the kitchen. He never smoked and took only the odd drink during the year, but Christmas Eve bowled him over.

Christmas Day in the parlour was a completely family day. Mossy, Mona and I played with our toys, the ones we had got in our stockings. We always played cards, games like Snap, and sometimes Pontoon. My father sang at the piano too, and this was when my mother showed her harmonising talent. Mossy and Mona were having music lessons from Aggie Quinn, and they played from their repertoire. I shall

Moore Street in the rare oul' times.

remember always the cosy comfortable feeling of those Christmas Days near the fire in our parlour. The feeling seemed to fade as I grew older, and I recall actually wishing it to remain. Christmas, however, was never Christmas without the Pantomime.

> 'Yez can keep your cowboy pictures,
> I can see them any day;
> I could do without me comic cuts
> Or a jaunt on Markey's dray.
> But there's one thing that I'd hate to miss,
> If I did, I'd feel, well, queer,
> It's when me father brins the family
> To the Pantomine each year.'

The pantomimes were to be seen in all of the theatres except the Theatre Royal. Our regular theatre was the Olympia, but we were brought also to the Tivoli and the Queens. In our own area, a Christmas panto was presented annually in the Father Mathew Hall in Church Street, and I remember going on three occasions with a crowd of boys to the Boys' Brigade Hall in Lower Church Street, near the old church of St. Michan's. The favourite panto was *Cinderella*.

Outside of the city theatres were to be found young hawkers with leaflets, which they waved as they shouted 'Pantomine Songs a Penny, Pantomine Songs a Penny.' And every year without fail came the fellow with the peaked cap who sang 'One of the Old Reserves' to the queues. The fellow who sang this song sometimes changed it to 'The Wreck of the Bugaboo', which was the story of a shipwreck or barge-wreck on the Grand Canal. I had heard him so often at the other theatre queues that I recall some of the lines:

> 'Come all you gentle hearted lads and listen unto me,
> I'll tell of my adventures upon the briny sea,
> Of the hardships and the dangers, the ones that I went
>   through
> When I shipped as cook and steward on board the
>   Bugaboo.'

The barrel-organ also made its appearance at the Pantomime queues and there was another regular with a mouth-organ who never played any tune but the one 'Show me the Way to go Home'. But the waiting seemed an eternity.

The 'old' Theatre Royal of the Twenties.

'At last the doors are opened,
Me father pays for all,
He takes young Gaby in his arms,
An' up the steps we crawl.
It's an awful journey upwards,
Though us kids go in 'leps',
But me mudder pants an' me father laughs,
An' he says, "Gerrup them steps".

At last we reach the gallery;
We rush down to the front,
Last year our Mossy slipped an' fell,
An' he got an awful dunt.
We sit down on our overcoats,
'Cause the seats are like cement,
An' then out loud we read and spell
Each big advertis'ment.

The conductor comes out smilin',
The lights go dim, then out,
The band strikes up a marchy tune,
An' someone starts to shout.
The curtain rises slowly,
We see a village green,
An' we all just sit there starin',
'Cause its like a lovely dream.

One year there was a 'divil',
An' he used to disappear;
A hole used open in the floor —
It made Hell seem awful near.
But the divil was fat and got stuck that night,
Though he tried to push and pull,
Then a voice from the gallery shouted out
"Three cheers, the place is full."

Me mother an' me father,
They love the Pantomine,
An' when the funny man appears,
They laugh at every line,
An' me mudder loves the music too,

Paddy as Mucky Dunn in the Theatre Royal 1952.

An' when a man appears,
Who sings ould songs like Nellie Dean,
Her eyes fill up with tears.'

The days after Christmas Day were happy days. Toys and dolls were brought out on the street to be boasted about:

'What's that?'
'A Meccano set. You can make hundreds of things with it.'
'They're on'y bits of tin. My father can get plenty of them tings.'
'What did you get?'
'I gorra bike.'
'Yeh bloody liar. Where is it?'
'Me mother wouldn't let me brin' it out.'
'Let's all go up to your house; we can see it there.'
'Me mother's gone out.'
'Yeh didn't ger' an'tin' in your stockin'.'
'You're another, I did.'
'Here's Cocky! What did *you* get?'
'I gorra shillin' an' an apple.'
'Tony gorra football — a real one.'
'Like one you have to pump up?'
'Yeh, one o' them. Let's ask Tony to come up to the Park . . . .'

We did our best to keep the grand feeling of Christmas alive as long as possible. I always hung up my stocking at Little Christmas Eve also (January 5), and never failed to get a penny or an orange in it.

Mulligan's of Stoneybatter (established 1792). Customers of days gone by.

20) Summer Holidays

A Wexford Rosary – Election fever – The Corporation Scholarship – Túirín Dubh – The Tailor and Ansty – Rumours from Dublin – Secondary School – The Arbour Hill boys.

MY BROTHER MOSSY had already spent many holidays in Wexford town, both during the last years of the First World War and during the Troubles. He even attended scnool there on the 'Old Pound', which faced Roche's Terrace, where my grandmother Crosbie lived. After the end of the Civil War I spent summer holidays there for three consecutive years. I travelled down by train from Harcourt Street Station on my own in July 1923. My grandmother lived at Number 1 Roches Terrace, and that is where I stayed each time. As I mentioned earlier she had been well known in her young days for her extraordinary singing voice. She was now very deaf and every night from her bed in the back room she called out the Rosary to Uncle Dick, Cousin Tony and myself in bed in the front room. Tony and Dick never answered, but being unable to hear them, she took it for granted that they did. Her Rosary, however, was very funny to hear, as she interspersed the phrases with questions and items of news:

> 'Hail Mary, full of Grace
> The Lord is with thee –
> Did you put out the dog, Tony –
> Blessed art thou –
> I hope you locked the back door –
> Amongst women
> And blessed is the fruit –
> That man from Taghmon called today Dick,
> I think it was about your bike –
> Of thy womb, Jesus.'

Old Túirín Dubh, Ballingeary (1927).

Cousin Tony and Uncle Dick used to be in stitches, but she kept on saying the decades. Even as I fell asleep, I could hear her still.

I loved Wexford, where I went catching bees near Wexford Park with John James, or swimming at Hore Rock with my cousin Jack Crosbie, or crossing the harbour to Ferrybank in Bung Potts' boat.

Back in Dublin the new State was taking its first faltering steps. When I came back to Dublin from my first holiday the city and country were getting ready for an election. It was the end of July and the summer was a scorching one. The Cumann na nGael party, led by William T. Cosgrave, won this and the new government set out to govern. The pace was slow, but there was peace in the country, and this took some getting used to.

It was three years later, that de Valera launched his 'soldiers of destiny'. In the election of 1927 Cosgrave's party lost many seats, but still managed to form a government. Kevin O'Higgins was assassinated in July, and there was another election in September. From this point on the Fianna Fáil party began to prosper.

The year 1926 was a year that changed many things for me. Besides the coming of radio and talkies an event occurred which altered my whole life. Brother Murray sent a batch of boys from our own school, Brunner, plus a batch each from St. Mary's Place, C.B.S. and O'Connell Schools down to Ballingeary in West Cork to study Irish. Most of us were Dublin Corporation Scholarship holders, the money from which paid for everything.

Five pounds paid for our return fare for a month plus board and lodgings plus Coláiste na Mumhan fees. We travelled by train to Cork City. From Glanmire we pushed our bikes and luggage across the city to a southside station where we boarded a train for Macroom. The carriage seats were most uncomfortable, being made of plain wood with no cushions. There was no such thing as a corridor on the train. Reaching Macroom, a car collected our bags, while we set off to cycle the rest of the way, seventeen miles.

That first year, there were not many in the group, but the following year the number swelled to about sixty. A picture of the group appeared in the monthly *An Lochrann*. Brother Murray was praised as the pioneer of the scheme and every year after 1926 the numbers grew. Among our early batch were the present auxiliary Bishop of Dublin, Dr. Joe Carroll, Andrias O Cuiv and Con Lehane. We lodged at Túirín Dubh with the Twomeys. This was a famous farmhouse, the one loved by Terence MacSwiney, who used cycle out from Cork just to spend weekends there. Jack Lynch and his brothers also stayed here in the Thirties. Other visitors at Túirín Dubh were Máire MacSwiney, Tomás MacCurtain, Erskine Childers (Sen.), Father Dominic and Father Albert, plus General Seán McKeon and Éamon de Valera. The house was raided dozens of times. All of the Twomeys took part in the Troubles. The old Fear a' Tí himself spent some time in jail during the days of the Land War.

From the back-streets of Dublin to the wild beauty of West Cork was a big jump for a boy. The countryside appeared as a fairyland to me, while the people were every bit as nice as our own Dubliners. My picture of the bogman began to change and my dearest friends there were Máire and Johnnie McCarthy, Dick Twomey and Lil, Cait Sweeney and Eileen. Also I made the acquaintance of the Tailor and Ansty long before the finger of publicity was pointed at them.

While staying in Ballingeary, we seemed cut off from the world outside. We had no newspapers and the radio had not made its presence felt as yet. In the early part of July 1927 a rumour reached the village that Kevin O'Higgins had been shot. It was some days before the rumour's truth was confirmed. The post came twice a week and I can remember waiting for almost three weeks, before I received a Postal Order for five shillings. About 1928 I had a letter from home telling me about the death of one of my Smithfield playmates, Patsy Devine. In an accident on Kingsbridge he had been thrown from a cart into the Liffey, where the thick mud rendered his rescue impossible.

The award of the Corporation Scholarship — value £130 — and my discovery of Ballingeary made the break with my early childhood friends inevitable. My mother made up her mind that I was to go on to Secondary School. Such a thing was unheard of among my street pals; they were all working at this time. Mossy left school on his fourteenth birthday to join the D.U.T. Co. and my sister Mona commenced work in the 'counting-house' of Clery & Co.

And so it happened, that I became a lone and lonely scholar, wending my way up Smithfield every morning, while all of my earlier chums settled down to working for a living. The only time we were to see each other now was at week-ends, and soon we began to lose touch completely, except for the occasional chance encounter on the street.

I did not realise it fully at the time, but I was coming to the end of my childhood. The climbing of roofs in Haymarket, the making of neat parcels of horse-dung for unsuspecting victims, running through the local pubs and shouting, calling names after the Market's characters, see-sawing on the hay-carts — all of these activities were braking to a stop. My future friends had to be school-going ones like myself. My ties with the boys of Stoneybatter grew stronger, as many of these had been in Ballingeary — Martin Daly, Johnny and Whacker Moore, Seamus Casey, Frank Delaney; there were others, who came from the St. Michan's and Arran Quay areas, such as Peadar Clifford, John Colgan, Denis Flanagan, Pat Cronin and Dick Harrington.

Unusual view of St. Michan's Church, the Four Courts dome and Jameson's famous chimney-stack.

21 Music Halls, Gramophones and Goodbye

Harro and Whacker — 'The Buildings' — Bottles for Danski — Olympia — The Chocolate Coloured Coon — Layton & Johnston — Our new gramophone — Jimmy O'Dea and Harry O'Donovan — Oct. 31st, 1930 — Goodbye to Oxmantown Green — And now.

MY SPECIAL NEW friends in the Stoneybatter area were Frank Harrington, known as Harro, and Paddy Moore, whom everybody knew as Whacker. Harro's parents had a restaurant in Parkgate Street and ran the Kiosk in the Phoenix Park. Whacker lived on Olaf Road; his Republican father had died as a result of ill-treatment by the British in Arbour Hill Jail. Another regular chum around this time was Frank Barron from Aughrim Street, whose father had an auctioneering business on Ormond Quay.

From 1926 my time in Dublin was filled playing football, hurling, handball, swimming and cycling. I got to know some boys from the local St. Gabriel's School also; the principal teacher here was Tomás O h-Aodha, who was a co-founder of the Gaelic League.

The maze of streets around and off Oxmantown Road — all of the houses were called artisan dwellings — was known to all and sundry as 'The Buildings!'. Before the scheme was built, the area, which included Arbour Hill, had been covered with apple trees. At an earlier period Arbour Hill had been famous for its oak trees, and it is said that many of the beams of Westminster Abbey in London come from the same hill.

The southern half of The Buildings was given a Danish period touch in the naming of the streets with names like Sitric Road, Sigurd Road, Olaf Road, Norseman Place, Viking Road etc. The main road through the scheme was and is Oxmantown Road, and it can be assumed that all of these names were used only in a gesture of recognition for the Danish influence on the north side of the Liffey.

The northern half of The Buildings is given an Irish geographical colour with place-names to the fore, names such as Ashford Street, Ben Edar Road, Carnew Street and so on. Many of the parents living in The Buildings were country-born and in the northern half lived quite a large number of British soldiers and their families. Very many of the menfolk also were employees of Arthur Guinness and Son.

About 1928 and 1929 I often went to the Olympia Theatre with Frank Harro and Whacker. As we had no money Frank brought us up to the Kiosk in the Phoenix Park, which his mother ran as a tea-rooms and place of refreshment. We gathered as many bottles and jars as we could and carried them in sacks down to Danski of North Brunswick Street. He bought the lot.

With this money we were able to see the show in the Olympia, and have chips afterwards on the way home in Cafolla's of Capel Street. All of the companies appearing in the Olympia at this time were British. There were two shows a night and they ran from Monday to Saturday. The last show on Saturday was always a bit rushed, as the artistes had to catch the mailboat back to England. G. H. Elliott, the Chocolate Coloured Coon, was still going strong at the end of the Twenties. His signature song was 'The Lily of Laguna', and 'Nellie Dean' was the song that 'made' Gertie Gitana. My father kept going to the stage shows; my mother began to go with him and to take an interest in the big names.

Names like Layton and Johnson were new, of course, to my father; he still hankered after the stars of the War years and the early Twenties. Yet, when Al Jolson burst on the scene in 1927, he welcomed him with open arms. The style of the comedian had changed during this decade. In my father's time, the comedian came out and sang comic songs and relied on movement and 'business' to raise laughs. The new comedian began to talk and to tell jokes, but he always commenced and finished with a song. So it wasn't a complete change.

Billy Bennett ('almost a gentleman') had a style of his own and was popular with young and old. He worked his gags into funny recitations and I can remember the audiences in stitches at some of his monologues e.g. 'She was pure as snow but she drifted. . . .' Shaun Glenville and Dorothy Ward were great favourites; they were still going strong in the Fifties when I myself appeared on the same bill with them in the Olympia.

When we got our gramophone in Kearney's of Capel Street in 1928, the most popular singers of the day were Layton and Johnston. They were coloured Americans, and they sang in harmony, with Turner Layton supplying the music on the piano. When they came to the old Theatre Royal in Dublin, the crowded audience clamoured for the songs which these two men made famous. The same songs were revived in later years, but these two harmonists were the original 'hit' singers. The songs were 'Are You Lonesome Tonight', 'Charmaine', 'Souvenirs', and 'Ramona'. The No. 1 song writer before the above arrived was Horatio Nichols. What with radio sets and gramophones things were looking up. My father bought records of Beniamino Gigli, Caruso and John McCormack, but he also purchased recordings of Harry Lauder and Old George Formby. And of course, we bought records of Jimmy O'Dea and Harry O'Donovan. A song I liked ended with:

'All the world will be bright
Next Saturday night.
When McGee draws his first week's pay.'

This was a song, sung by Harry, about a poor family, and the wonderful effect on the family when the father got his first job. It was a song of the period that had just passed, for we were now at the end of the Twenties.

Meanwhile in the immediate area of Smithfield and Haymarket life went on as before, almost. The hay-market days were still Tuesdays and Fridays, and the cattle market day was still Thursday. There was still a large number of horses to be seen, but some of the farmers were now bringing in their hay on lorries. It was the beginning of the end. Men and women became more clothes conscious. Shirts were now being bought in boxes that brought three loose collars with them. The Charleston dance had arrived, Al Jolson was singing, the Ardna-crusha Hydro-electric station was functioning, the talkies had come to some of the cinemas, Éamon de Valera had gone into the Dáil, we had loudspeaker radios, Gene Tunney had beaten the unbeatable Jack

Northern end of Stoneybatter leading to Prussia Street and Aughrim Street.

Martin (Mossy) Crosbie and Danny Cummins (comedian) in the early Forties in O'Connell Street.

Dempsey, girls were getting their hair bobbed, gold and silver fáinnes were to be seen everywhere, the céilidhe dances in the Mansion House and 25 Parnell Square were packed and a man named Matt Talbot had died.

When 1930 arrived I was six feet tall, with most of my interest directed to games of handball and hurling. I still walked up Smithfield with my school-books, through an area that looked on me as an overgrown schoolboy, which I was. And then one night — it was October 30th, 1930 — my family and I bid a sad goodbye to 12A Bridewell Lane and Oxmantown Green.

EPILOGUE

And Now . . .

Although the family left the old Markets area in 1930, I continued to keep in touch. I kept up my connections with the Stoneybatter area, and from 1934 down to the present, I have passed through the Smithfield area twice a day on my way to and from Brunner, this time as a teacher.

The once horse-packed width of Smithfield and Haymarket is now machine packed. Old cars, new cars, and broken-down vehicles of every kind desecrate the scene. Number seven in the Haymarket remains unchanged, but Robert Emmet's depot was demolished and rebuilt, the only gesture to what had been there lies in the imitation Georgian front to the house. The tenement houses of Queen Street are gone, but the words 'St. Paul's Free School' are still there on the wall.

I have witnessed the complete change with a feeling of sadness. Shops that were the backcloth to our boyhood acting are no more. If requested, I am sure that Billy Harmon, senior, of Bourkes, the Funeral Undertakers, could call out the long list of Dubliners who walked, danced, ran, fought, loved, quarrelled, cursed, sang, and died on Oxmantown Green. May the Good Lord have mercy on all their souls, and may we all laugh heartily together some day in that celestial abode, when a shrill voice calls: *Your Dinner's Poured Out.*

214

Queen Street tenements as they were. Taken from Blackhall Place.

Paddy receiving a Jacob's Award from Hilton Edwards (1964).

Front page of *The Irish Independent* January 19, 1979:

CORPORATION PLANS TO CLOSE
SMITHFIELD MARKET

Dublin's Smithfield Market is to be closed to make way for major urban redevelopment in the area over the next few years.

An action plan for the area is being prepared by Dublin Corporation to complement future development there, including a new court complex for the Department of Justice and a new headquarters for Irish Distillers.

A market has existed in Smithfield since 1665, when Dublin Corporation devoted a portion of its estate, then called Exmantown Green, to the use of the public as a large market for the sale of hay, straw, cattle and pigs.

In recent years, however, the area has been little used as a market except for the limited sale of straw, hay and vegetables. Part of it has been designated by the Government as a lorry park.

The Corporation's housing scheme at Friary Avenue, which abuts onto the east side of Smithfield, has been completed. Irish Distillers plan to redevelop their property on the same side to provide for their new headquarters.

The Department of Justice is considering a court complex near the new distillery headquarters. To cater for this the Corporation's planning department is preparing an action plan for the entire Smithfield area, including a new road pattern.

Yesterday, the Corporation's finance committee heard a report on the plan and gave full backing to closure of Smithfield as a market. The matter will come before the next meeting of the City Council.

APPENDIX

Phrases from the Markets Area and a short glossary of Dublin slang words:

You big long mother's rarin'! (name-calling).
You big long drink of water! (name-calling).
She is very old, but she has all her facilities.
She's in very bad humour — like a bag of cats.
You hoor's melt (usually used in a slanging match).
Go home and tell your mother to get married.
That snotty nosed little cnat!
He'd shit in your parlour and charge you for it (mean fellow).
He's a bit of a molly (effeminate).
That fella is as wide as a gate, i.e. cute.
May you die roarin' like Doran's ass! (a curse).
I wanna do me number two (child's voice).
   Do it in your hand and throw it out the windah. (mother's voice).
That bockedy-arsed oul' bitch!
He'd talk the teeth off a saw.
A shave, a shampoo and a shite and I'm a new man.
That fella's a right cur.

(The language of the Dublin Markets Area was coarse and vulgar, but the now famous four-letter word had not taken over the vocabulary yet.)

He's gone for his tea (anyone killed or after dying).
Your eyes are bigger nor your belly (a greedy one).
He bet him as black as a mourning coach.
He has a face like the Earl of Hell's arse (ugly).
He's very *handy* with his *feet.*
There was laughin' and curran'y cake and talkin' to girls (a good party).
Don't be actin' the maggot (messing).
They're like arse-holes, sure everybody has them (when there was a plentiful supply).
If the wind blows you'll be left that way (if a boy 'turned' his eyes).
He hadn't a flitter on him (no clothes).
You have no call to that (no claim or right).
I'd like me job (that is, no, I won't).
I wouldn't bother me arse about that (something not worth considering).
Goin' around like a constipated greyhound. (Down in the dumps, glum)

218

As fit as a cello (an improvement on the fiddle).
As scarce as hobby-horse manure.
I will in me hat, i.e. I won't do it.
It was the rale Ally Daly (the genuine article).
He'd live in your ear and sublet your ear-drum (a mean fellow).
If bull-shit was music, that fellow'd be a brass band.
He's like the barber's cat, full of wind and piss. (All talk and no action)
She's as white as a maggot.
As ignorant as a bag of arses.
As fat as a bishop.
There's no use in bein' iggerant unless you can show it.
One wit more and he'd be a half-wit.
He wouldn't give you the steam off his piss (a mean fellow).
He has an eye like a stinkin' eel (he watches everything).
Do you want your snot broke? (Are you looking for a fight.)
Do you want your eye dyed? (Are you looking for a fight.)
She has a face like the back of a cab, i.e. ugly.
That fellow'll be late for his own funeral (slow).
That one is so mean she puts the butter on the bread with a feather
and takes it off again with a razor.
He thinks he's the cat's pyjamas, i.e. perfect.
Sure it was like throwin' apples into an orchard, i.e. doing some-
thing stupid.
I nearly had a canary (with fright or shock).
A little fart of a fella (small).
I knew him when he hadn't an arse to his trousers.
She's no oil-painting, i.e. not very pretty.
He was fit to be tied, i.e. mad, angry.
He'd lick it off a sore leg, i.e. fond of drink.
He arsed his way through the crowd.
She'd eat you out of house and home (big appetite).
It gave me the hump, i.e. bored me.
Cold and stiff, like a frozen snot.
There's only one head bigger than Joe's and that's Bray Head.
That's an awful mornin'; it looks as if it has been up all night.
He ran like a hairyman, i.e. very fast.
As small as a mouse's diddy.
He's half a cocker and half a conger eel (a mongrel dog).
That fella'd skin a fart, i.e. do anything for money.
Where would yeh be goin' an' no bell on your bike (used in conver-
sation like: I ask you).
As pretty as Pamela (Lord Edward Fitzgerald's wife, maybe!).

A GLOSSARY OF SOME DUBLIN SLANG TERMS

aytin house *restaurant*
babby *a baby*
beaver *a beard*
bellier *a flat dive*
biff *a slap in school*
bobby *policeman*
bowsy *scoundrel*
bowler *a dog*
boxing the fox *robbing an orchard*
bronical *bronchial*
bum freezer *a short coat*
bummer *a toucher*
burgoo *porridge*
Caddy *Catechism*
chaney *broken bit of delf*
chiseler *a young boy*
clickin' mots *chasing girls*
clod *a penny*
to cog *to copy*
combo *football practice*
crock *an old bicycle*
crulety *cruelty*
cut *appearance*
dawny *sick looking*
decko *a look*
deuce *twopence*
dickied out *dressed up*
diddy *breast*
doorsteps *thick slices of bread*
ecker *home exercise*
fanner *a fellow who won't work*
to feck *to steal*
folleyed *followed*
fudge *a farthing*
gardener *Park Ranger*
gargle *drink*
geyser *a cat*
gollier *a spittle*
goyno *money*
great gas *good fun*
to greg *to tantalise*

grush *money thrown*
hardchaw *a harum scarum*
a hardroot *a devil-may-care*
haut *hit (past tense)*
hop *a dance*
jow off *buzz off*
to ler on *pretend*
longers *long trousers*
lugged *dragged by the ear*
make *a ha'penny*
me oul' fella *my father*
me oul' wan *my mother*
mebs *marbles*
mongler *mongrel*
mosey *a stroll*
mot *woman or girlfriend*
musicianer *musician*
to nark *to complain*
on the jare *mitching*
an ould bar *a song*
oul' rip *a spiteful person*
an oul' wan *a woman*
out on gur *staying away from home*
a restitution *a recitation*
rozzer *a policeman*
a rucky up *a row*
ruggy *a row*
a scut *a small fellow*
a slug *a mouthful*
spar *boxing stance*
stabber *cigarette butt*
to stag *to betray*
to stand out *to fight*
stookawn *a fool*
swalleyed *swallowed*
varnishing cream *vanishing cream*
whitenin' *whiting*
wing *a penny*
a young wan *a girl*

220

SOURCES

James Collins *Life in Old Dublin* James Duffy & Co. 1913
Michael Corcoran *Dublin Trams* Dublin Corporation Newsletter No. 37
1978
Rev. Dillon Cosgrave O. Carm. *North Dublin City* Four Courts Papers
1977
Most Rev. N. Donnelly, D.D. *History of Dublin Parishes*
Wilmot Harrison *Memorable Dublin Houses* Yorkshire S.R.V. 1971
John Harvey *Dublin* S. R. Publishers 1972
Rev. C. T. McCreedy *Dublin Street Names* Carraig Books 1975.
John A. Murphy *Ireland in the 20th Century* Gill & Macmillan 1975
David Neligan *The Spy in the Castle* McGibbon and K. 1968.
Desmond Ryan *The Rising* Golden Eagle Books 1966.
School Annals C.B.S., Nth. Brunswick St.

Thanks

We would like to thank the following for providing us with photo-
graphs: John Jameson — The Irish Times (per John Boyle and Arthur
Gill) 16 and 17; Engineering Dept., Dublin Corporation 77, 150, 151,
cover; Wm. McLoughlin, late of Hanlon's, N.C. Rd. 86; Edward
Keating, Hanover Tce., Brighton 70, 98; Paddy Mulligan, Stoneybatter,
Dublin 7 200, 201; Desmond Cummins, Strawberry Hall 45, 164; Chas.
Heather, Arran Quay, Dublin 7 147; James Kirwan, Ard Ri Road,
Dublin 7 71; Billy Harmon, Bourke's, Queen Street, Dublin 7 75; Pat
Doyle Alderwood Close, Tallaght 96; Guinness Museum 108; Old
Dublin Society 162; Pat Johnston, Civic Museum 162; Pat Doyle,
Laburnum Road, Dublin 14 42; W. Lawrence Collection, National
Library 68, 115, 135, 159, 192, 183; Eason Collection, National
Library 196; Keogh Collection, National Library 83; George Gmelch
14, 22, 47, 82, 101, 106, 118, 120, 124, 173; Capuchin Annual 60;
Guinness Museum 108; Mrs. Eileen Tyrrell, Nth. Brunswick Street,
Dublin 7 178.

Index

SILVERMINING IN QUEEN STREET (1922)

Hobby was there;
He saw it fall,
The half-crown from his pocket,
As the wavering, drunken man
Tightrope-walked his way along the path.
It plopped into the cellar
Of Dinny Gogan's shop,
Through the grating near the door.
And so, with wire and tin,
All three of us lay down to fish
Through the narrow iron grill
For the silver down below.
Three times the wanted, lovely coin
Was almost in our grasp;
Three times it slid away.
But now once more the bent, tin scoop
Had raised the brightness towards us.
Suddenly, an arm appeared,
A snake-like slender arm,
Out from the cellar darkness,
And picking up our precious, shiny jewel,
Whipped it from our sight.

Paddy Crosbie